90 DAY INSTAGRAM
CONTENT PLANNER

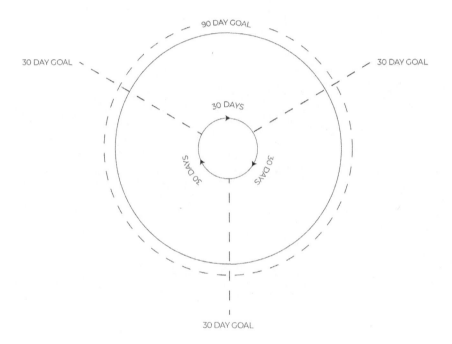

THIS PLANNER BELONGS TO:

CONTENTS

ABOUT THE CREATOR

Hey! This is me, Inge; it's pronounced like 'singer', 'ringer' or even 'minger!' I am an enthusiastic and ambitious self confessed digital marketing and Instagram addict. I love all things figuring out how to use digital marketing to my advantage; and manipulating and moulding the way it works to turn businesses into successful and profitable things!

I have been an entrepreneur/ business owner all my life - I feel like those two words are interchangeable and I call myself one of the other on different days depending on how I feel so i'ma let you choose which one suits me best. But yeah seriously all my life I've been hustling to make a little extra cash and do something different. It started as hosting talent shows and pop up stalls outside of my house selling my old toys when I was around the age of 7 and then blossomed into something I could call a 'proper' business between the ages of 17-19 when I used to sell homemade cocktails on the street in milkshake cartons! Yes I was underage and unlicensed - but I did it anyway!

Years passed and I worked my way through a host of small businesses including a pop up mobile cocktail bar and event management & wedding planning; all the while studying for my business management and marketing degree and side lining in various hospitality establishments and marketing agencies. Then fast forward 10 years and people started to ask me how I had built my business and how I knew so much about regularly attracting clients and the answer was simple - Instagram!

I now spend my days helping passionate business owners like you boost their visibility, grow their sales and expand their business potential through the power of Instagram and digital media - all with a highly strategic approach. I'll help you grow your digital footprint - so you can not only have a larger audience, but a more engaged, responsive and quality consumer base. I am proud to say that to date I have consulted over 1000 businesses ranging from corporate to start up and product to service based and everything in between; on how to harness the power of Instagram and digital marketing strategy. I regularly host webinars and trainings to speak on the power of Instagram and have been described as an authority figure on the future and power of digital media for SMEs in the UK - yes me! That mad girl who thought it was okay to shake up a long island iced tea and sell it on the street!

This 90 day content planner is my own little love letter to you to pour some time and strategy into your business and do the work. Yes a 'normal' love letter would shower you with compliments and good vibes - but in reality that won't do a thing in moving your business forwards if you're not taking the steps. So I guess this is a little tough love and a little bit of let's pull out our fingers and get the work done.

I want you to commit to this and really go for it over the next 90 days. I want you to do the things you intend to do and then I want you to reap the rewards of your consistency and your strategic messaging. Because believe me it will work! And then I want you to do the same over the next 90 days and the next after that. So on and so forth. Because the secret to business success isn't some leprechaun at the end of the rainbow or just 'good luck' and 'big audiences'. It's about showing up, doing the work, marketing your business and being consistent about it. Far beyond the point where it makes you cry and fills you with doubt. And well beyond the days when you give up and feel like you wanna take a day off. This 90 day content planner is your guide to success. Follow it and you will make a difference to your business and by proxy a difference to your lifestyle - because we all wanna be rolling in the good stuff!

THE CUSTOMER JOURNEY

90 DAY CONCEPT

Ask any business owner what they are working on and you'll get a whole load of responses. Some people will have their whole 5 year plan mapped out to the finest details and some will only be planning one week in advance. To make sure you stay on track and stay focused on your goals and your growth the optimum amount of time to make detailed plans is in a 90 day cycle.

90 days is long enough for you to make serious moves in your business but not too long to become unmanageable and unrealistic to stick to. There are 12 months in a year and when you break this down into 4 quarters there are on average 90 days per quarter so this gives you the opportunity to plan for seasonal changes in your business, stay ahead of yourself and hit your targets.

The other benefit to 90 day planning is that you can catch anything that goes wrong rather quickly and fast forward on areas where you are improving and be able to track back to where those positive and negative changes came from. Plus my signature launch & campaign content neatly fits into a 90 days cycle and that's what we are here for so let me explain what you need to do next...

BUYERS JOURNEY

In business it's important to understand a standard customer journey and apply this to your marketing and your messaging so that you can be sure you are attracting, nurturing and selling consistently to your customers.

A standard customer journey follows the pattern:
Awareness, Consideration, Purchase, Retention, Advocacy.

You bought this planner because you're focused on the first part on the customer journey - making the moolah! So this is where we are going to zone in on. Generally to improve on the retention and advocacy phases you've gotta do a really hot job on the sale (which is on you and your business). But my special powers with this planner come in on the Consideration stage of the customer journey, essentially turning new followers into clients and customers so let's break these down.

To move someone through the journey towards the purchase we are going to keep things simple. First they've got to **KNOW** about you; then they've got to **LIKE** you; they have to **TRUST** you; And only then may they be interested in **BUYING FROM YOU**. And surprise, surprise when it comes to Instagram and social media this process takes around 3 months on average! Perfect to slot into 90 days... See what I'm getting at here?!

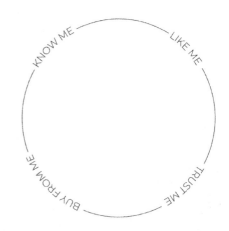

KNOW ME

Is not about telling strangers your name. The know me stage of the journey is designed to help people move from knowing you exist to liking you. They know you exist already and they are aware of what you do otherwise they wouldn't be following you. Now is your time to lean in on what makes you and your business unique. Tell us all about your values, what you stand for and why you do what you do rather than anything else! You'll have all the prompt for this later on in the planner but remember you're not talking to strangers here, you're talking to acquaintances and trying to turn them into friends.

LIKE ME

Like me isn't actually about trying to make people like you. It's actually the opposite. You are trying to put people off who aren't right for you and by proxy will make your perfect people love you even more. Now is your chance to stand out from the crowd. Tell us why you are different, tell us what drives you and motivates you; tell us what changes you want to make and how you want to impact the world. Get passionate, get real and make us like you and your business.

TRUST ME

If people don't trust you they won't buy from you. The exchange of money is an exchange of trust. When someone purchases from you they are saying that they want to exchange their time and effort for something you have. No matter which way you wing it there is always emotion tie up in the exchange of money, it might be positive emotion or negative but whichever way you gottta make them trust you before they'll hand it over. You could share the obvious here, testimonials, reviews, feedback etc. but you could also tell stories about how amazing your clients and customers are, you could talk us through your own journey of entrepreneurship and describe your qualification or life experience. Like I said, we will get to the prompts later but you get where I'm coming from.

BUY FROM ME

If you aren't asking for the sale you won't make the sale. Most business owners are great at the passive sale but when it comes to asking their leads to put their hands in their pockets they wobble and don't directly ask for the sale. You need to sell. It's part of owning a business. So in the sales section of this journey you're going to have to get uncomfortable. You're going to have to push yourself out of your comfort zone and ask for that sale; and I'll help you do it!

Stick with the Know, Like, Trust & Buy From Me
joourney and by the end of the next 90 days you'll be so
comfortable with your marketing and your messaging
that you'll want to do it all over again in the next 90 days
after that!

Now that you're feeling confident on the theory behind
this content planner let's move forwards to look at how
to actually fill out the pages. Use these next sections as
references as you move through the book.

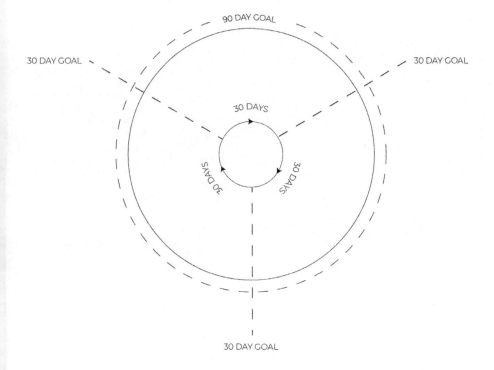

HOW TO SET YOUR 90 DAY GOAL

This is your longest goal you'll be setting in this planner. Make sure it's reasonable and achievable. My suggestion is to make a single focused goal on one section of your business rather than trying to cover all bases. Set yourself a sales or target driven goal and use that to inspire you to create other goals that will help you achieve this.

ONE

You'll see that the 90 day goal pages enable you to set up your own 90 day calendar. Do this first before you do anything else. Set out a start date and an end date for yourself to stick to. There is no use in giving yourself a time span, you want exact dates and a specific timeline to work towards. Maybe you're starting tomorrow, maybe it's on Monday, perhaps you're starting next month. Whatever date you begin on, fill out the weekly grid with the dates so that you know what you're sticking to.

TWO

Write your big goal and make it SMART. And when I say SMART I don't mean intelligent goals, I mean Specific, Measurable, Achievable, Realistic and Timely goals. You are more likely to achieve SMART goals because you have spent time analysing the specifics of your goal.

So write your big 90 day goal and then think to yourself:
Is this a SPECIFIC goal?
Can I MEASURE this goal with stats?
Is this goal ACHIEVABLE and REALISTIC in 90 days?
Have I given myself a TIME frame in which to complete this goal?

THREE

Break this goal down a little further and really flesh it out to make sure you get to know what you're working towards. I want you to stop and reflect on a few things here. What is it you are hoping to achieve with this goal? Do you have a specific financial goal in mind with this? How much impact would you like to achieve in the next 90 days and what does that look like? How will you feel over the next 90 days and what specifically are you selling in the next 90 days?

FOUR

Once you've explored your 90 day goal in detail you need to move onto the calendar pages of the 90 day goals and plot in your dates you have set and anything significant that is happening over the next 90 days so that you can plan for it. Birthdays, business events, holidays etc. Anything that may help or hinder you in your quest for 90 day success so that you can be aware of things before they pop up.

FIVE

Tracking your stats is imperative to tracking how well you are doing. There's no guessing game going on here. Let's see how consistent you are at the moment and use that as a benchmark for your consistency moving forwards. The key to success here is to stick to every day of your 90 day content plan so we need to do a little stats housekeeping before we get going. Head to the insights in your Instagram account and do a little thinking around what you are posting and how you are interacting with potential customers and people that will help you to grow your business.

SIX

Set yourself a growth percentage. This is highly individual to you and is something that you will need to track across multiple 90 day cycles to make sure you are consistent across the year. The specific insights you could measure on Instagram are:

Reach — How many strangers and current followers are actually seeing you week in and week out.

Profile Visits — How many people are interested in you enough on Instagram to come back to your account and look for more information?

Follows — How well your audience is growing and how many potential leads are you attracting into your Instagram space - please note it is percentage growth, not total number. Total number isn't something we are going to focus on here; it's all about growth!

Content Interactions — How well is your content nurturing people and encouraging them to interact and pay attention to you?

Website Taps — How many people are taking the big step to check out your website or head to a different digital space off of Instagram to seek out more information about you? This is an important stat to track.

SEVEN

Pause a moment before you get into it and imagine how amazing it's going to feel when you stick to this plan. I'm not super woo but I know that visualisation is an important part of the business process. If you can imagine it, and feel it and think it's possible, then subconsciously you will do everything in your power to move yourself towards that reality. I've worked with enough people to know that when they start to talk down to themselves or don't believe in themselves the success just won't happen because they are forcing it to move away from them. So take some time out on the visualisation pages to just do a little thinking about how amazing you are and how amazing this journey is going to be. And if not for anything then just for a little written reminder of how far you go when you look back on yourself in 90 days time.

HOW TO FILL EACH 30 DAY GOAL

Each 30 days in a 90 day cycle then needs to be broken down in order to make the whole goal achievable. You are not going to be able to do everything at once; and you need to allow yourself to concentrate on specific areas of your goal at one time. If you want to keep things simple then think about your 30 day cycles like this:

--- 1ST CYCLE ---

Growth & Awareness

Those first 30 days of a 90 day goal are where you need to zone in on attracting new strangers to your business; get people to know you exist, and use organic or paid audience growth strategies to grow your following.

--- 2ND CYCLE ---

Nurturing & Consideration

The next 30 days are to nurture and warm up your current leads. Your goal here isn't to grow anymore. Any growth that happens in these next 30 days is a bonus but I want you to zone in on who is currently interested in you and who is already there instead of chasing the strangers. And you need to start warming them up and encouraging them to take more action with you.

--- 3RD CYCLE ---

Selling

The last 30 days cycle is for selling. This is your purchase zone. These 30 days are dedicated solely to selling and turning that warm audience into customers and clients. Your messaging in these last 30 days is all concentrated on your sales and it's time for you to laser focus on your hot leads.

To make this easy for you, every 30 days you'll see space in the content planner for you to stop, reflect and plan ahead. In these pages you need to do the following:

1. Set out your dates for the next 30 days and write down your 30 day goal; don't forget to make it SMART!
2. Set your intentions, give yourself key numerical targets to work towards so that you are able to track your progress.
3. Note down anything else you may need to do for the next 30 days to keep yourself on track or pay attention to.

WHAT STATS TO TRACK

Handily there are 5 key Instagram insights you can use to track this whole process and keep you on the ball with your 90 day plan. There's not shooting into the blind in this book; oh no! I want you to make sure you are going to hit your targets by tracking your stats. You need to turn strangers into sales on Instagram so I want you to keep an eye on the following 5 areas:

Reach
This is how many strangers you are in front of in a given time period. The higher this is the better. And if it's consistently improving week on week this is awesome! Make sure your Reach is at its highest in your 1st 30 day cycle.

Profile Visits
How often are you encouraging people to check you out? How much of that Reach are you actually turning into someone taking the conscious effort to have a look through your profile? (There may be current followers included in your profile visit insight - but the more people that have a look over your account the better) This needs to be growing week on week but especially in that first 30 day cycle

Follows
Not total followers! I'll repeat that! We aren't looking for that total follower fluctuation, we are looking to see how many of those profile visits are converting into actual followers. How many new people are taking the conscious action with you to opt into hearing more about what you do? You want to either see a steady number or increase here, especially in that first 30 day cycle.

Content Interactions
This tells you exactly how interesting your people find you, how much they relate to you and what they want to see more of from you. Never ever neglect your content interactions because they reveal all. The total number of content interactions is a sum of all of the actions someone could take with your posts and stories in a given time period. You want this to increase week on week. But beyond just the number you also need to pay close attention to which content is creating the increase in content interactions. Zone in on your best performing content and make more of that. Not only will you warm up your audience more effectively if you give them more of what they want; but you will grow faster. This is a great insight to pay attention to in the second 30 day cycle.

Website Taps
Alert alert! Someone wants to do more than just mindlessly browse your instagram reel. They actually want to learn more about you, take action with you and check you out. Website taps are the bees knees. This means that you have warmed someone up enough for them to take a moment out of their day and browse through your website link. You're doing a great job! Ideally these need to steadily increase throughout the whole 90 day cycle whilst you are attracting and warming up potential leads but then will dramatically increase in that last 30 day cycle when you are making the sale.

OPTIONAL EXTRA...

Why you need to track who to mute and unmute.

And I wanna throw in an option sixth thing that's specific to Instagram and your success in the next 90 days and that is 'muting people on Instagram'. Let's be honest; everyone's out there trying to live their best life on Instagram and that can be distracting and downright disheartening on a bad day. If you let those comparison demons or jealousy gremlins get into your brain when you're trying to grow your business it will throw you off. So don't let it.

If you find yourself coming off of Instagram and feeling worse than when you logged on then you need to take a little conscious action and actively think about what has made you feel worse. Which account were you looking at that made you doubt yourself and is it happening often? If this is happening on the regular then you need to do something about it and use the mute button.

You don't have to go knees in and unfollow the account but perhaps putting people on mute for a little while will help you find your head space again, get you back in the driver's seat and focused on achieving your goals. They won't know you've muted them (unless you tell them!) and you can keep your Instagram account an uplifting and positive space for yourself. And you can always unmute people once you're feeling a little stronger.

10 DAY CHECK IN

Staying in touch with your ebbs and flows in your content can be very helpful to enable you to shift and adjust your approach depending on what is performing well and what isn't doing too great. Once every 10 days you will be asked to check in. Note down your key stats and reflect on which content is doing well and what may need to be improved on. Be sure to not only get statistical about this but also try to think about why you may be seeing fluctuations here and there. What energy did you come with? What happened in the news that week? Have people been offline a lot recently? Or why did that post go viral? What was it about it that people liked?

HOW TO FILL OUT EACH DAY OF THE 90 DAY PLANNER

Now that you've got all your goals set, it's time to tackle this planner day by day. You'll notice there is space for you to track the day you are on and prompts for you to use to inspire your content for every single day of the 90 day content planner. These prompts are broken down into the know, like, trust and buy from me messaging cycle we have discussed earlier on in this book.

I want you to flesh out these prompts, make them individual to you and think about how you can really drive that message home. Not only do I want you to think about the caption you may write, but what's the point of each post and how does it add value to a followers day? You can also pause to think about what the best format is for each post you create because each posting feature on Instagram is good for different kinds of messaging, perhaps you could drive the message home with a post or a reel; cool infographic or perhaps you need to go live, or do a story to explain what you'd like to say? Whichever messaging format you think your followers would enjoy and interact with the most.

Once you are finished for the day then track what's gone on and keep in touch with any key conversations you have been having or anyone of interest you have connected with. As a bonus I have included some sales tracking sheets to the back of this planner for you to have a dedicated space to keep a tally of your sales and any leads you are collecting along your way.

During the first two 30 day cycles the focus is on attracting and nurturing followers and then the last 30 day cycle is for selling. You'll notice in the planner that the language and the prompts shift between these cycles. The prompts and reflections are a lot more sales based and direct in the last 30 days; so give yourself the permission to really go for it and push yourself out of your comfort zone to amass those sales.

ADVICE ON HOW TO STICK TO THE 90 DAY PLANNER

Planning is the best bit of this 90 day planner. The hard part is sticking to it. Yeah I'm talking to you over there with the beautifully written plan with the different colour coded notes, sticky pads and highlighters. That's great but it's going to mean poop if you can't keep to your own plan. I love planning, so much so that I made a planning book all about planning your 90 day plans! But I'll be the first to admit that sticking to it is tricky. Shiny new ideas pop up; life gets in the way and suddenly you're staring down the barrel of the next quarter wondering where the hell the last 3 months went! So here are a few practical things that I do to keep myself accountable and on track.

TIME-BLOCK YOUR DIARY

Yeah this is more planning! But breaking down those 7 day cycles into daily actionable tasks and then setting aside dedicated time to actually do them will help you stick to your plans and bring you closer to achieving your goals.

BUDDY UP

I have a fantastic group of peers and mentors who I know will call me out on my bs if I start swaying from the plan. Telling yourself why you didn't do something is easy; telling someone else about all of the things that got in your way from you doing what you set out to do is hard; they'll judge you! And you need that fear of judgement to make sure you stay on the straight and narrow!

PLAN IN ADVANCE

That's right! Actively setting time aside to plan out your next 90 days in advance and getting the goals filled out, setting your 30 and 7 day cycles and consciously going through the motions will help you stick to it. Setting aside time to plan in advance helps you consciously set the mood for the next 90 days and helps you seal your mindset when it comes to achieving your goals.

TRACK YOUR MOOD

There will be times when you don't want to stick to it. You may even want to jack it all in some days whilst buzzing like you've sealed the best ever business deal other days. Have you ever considered that there may be a cycle to these fluctuations in your approach to your business. Personally, my hormones rule my life and by proxy my business and so it has become a priority to track my mood and ensure that any business decisions and consistency slumps are down to hormone changes and nothing else. It could be finances, it could be food, it could be days of the week or even other people that affect your ability to perform in your business. If there's a chance your mood changes could be impacting your bottom line then track them and stay ahead and on top of these changes.

CHANGE YOUR SCENERY

Do you find yourself staring at the same 4 walls day in and day out? It could be time to change things up. Perhaps consider working from a coffee shop a couple of days a week or booking yourself into a co-working space every so often. Do as I do and find a swanky hotel that inspires you and do all of your content planning and marketing activities from there so that you can feel your best and feel inspired when you're creating. It's important that your content comes from a positive and uplifting space so that it will come across in this way.

BATCH YOUR CONTENT CREATION, PHOTOS & VIDEO

There's nothing worse than having to be creative, inspiring, thoughtful and strategic all on the fly. In fact there's no way you will be able to make your best content all day every day and still be able to perform all of your other business tasks. The best thing you can do for yourself and for your plans is to create your content in batches. Dedicate a couple of days a month to organising your posts and a few hours every week writing them up and posting them out. You'll feel better for it, you'll be more prepared and you'll be more likely to stick to your plan.

WHAT WILL YOU DO?

_____

_____

_____

_____

_____

_____

_____

_____

_____

_____

_____

_____

_____

_____

Your 90 Day Goal...

M T W T F S S / WEEK 1 2 3 4 5

JAN FEB MAR APR MAY JUN JUL AUG SEP OCT NOV DEC

WRITE YOUR GOAL HERE

─── FILL OUT YOUR 90 DAY CYCLE ───

Complete the calendars below by plotting your start and end date.

M   T   W   T   F   S   S   M   T   W   T   F   S   S

M   T   W   T   F   S   S   M   T   W   T   F   S   S

WHAT WOULD YOU LIKE TO ACHIEVE?

YOUR FINANCIAL GOAL

YOUR IMPACT GOAL

HOW DO YOU WANT TO FEEL ABOUT
YOUR BUSINESS IN 90 DAYS?

WHAT WILL YOU BE SELLING OVER
THE NEXT 90 DAYS?

QUARTER PLAN VIEW

30	DATE	NOTES	60	DATE	NOTES
1			1		
2			2		
3			3		
4			4		
5			5		
6			6		
7			7		
8			8		
9			9		
10			10		
11			11		
12			12		
13			13		
14			14		
15			15		
16			16		
17			17		
18			18		
19			19		
20			20		
21			21		
22			22		
23			23		
24			24		
25			25		
26			26		
27			27		
28			28		
29			29		
30			30/60		

NOTES

90	DATE	NOTES
1		
2		
3		
4		
5		
6		
7		
8		
9		
10		
11		
12		
13		
14		
15		
16		
17		
18		
19		
20		
21		
22		
23		
24		
25		
26		
27		
28		
29		
30/90		

TRACK YOUR BEGINNING STATS

M T W T F S S / WEEK 1 2 3 4 5

JAN FEB MAR APR MAY JUN JUL AUG SEP OCT NOV DEC

1 2 3 4 5 6 7 8 9 10 11 12 13 14 15 16 17
18 19 20 21 22 23 24 25 26 27 28 29 30 31

HOW MANY POSTS ARE YOU DOING A WEEK?

HOW MANY PEOPLE ARE YOU CONNECTED WITH
THAT WILL HELP YOUR BUSINESS?

HOW MANY DAYS A WEEK ARE
YOU POSTING STORIES?

HOW MUCH TIME DO YOU SPEND INTER-
ACTING, NOT BROWSING?

WHAT PERCENTAGE GROWTH ARE YOU
HOPING TO ACHIEVE THIS MONTH?

VISUALISATION

HOW WILL YOU FEEL IF YOU STICK
TO YOUR 90 DAY PLAN?

FREEWRITE...

Talent and inspiration will only get you so far...

...consistency and habits will build a business.

Your First 30 Day Goal

M T W T F S S / WEEK 1 2 3 4 5

JAN FEB MAR APR MAY JUN JUL AUG SEP OCT NOV DEC

M   T   W   T   F   S   S

WRITE YOUR GOAL HERE

HOW MANY POSTS DO YOU
WANT TO MAKE A WEEK?

HOW MANY PEOPLE DO YOU WANT TO CONNECT
WITH THAT WILL HELP YOUR BUSINESS?

HOW MANY DAYS A WEEK DO
YOU PLAN TO POST STORIES?

1ST 30 DAY CYCLE - MONTH VIEW

HOW MUCH TIME WILL YOU SPEND INTERACTING, NOT BROWSING?

WHAT PERCENTAGE GROWTH ARE YOU HOPING TO ACHIEVE THIS MONTH?

ANY OTHER GOALS?

FREEWRITE...

(FIRST) 30 DAY CYCLE

M T W T F S S / WEEK 1 2 3 4 5

1 2 3 4 5 6 7 8 9 10 11 12 13 14 15 16 17
18 19 20 21 22 23 24 25 26 27 28 29 30 31

YOU ARE IN **KNOW ME**, HERE'S A PROMPT:
What kind of people do you love to help?

———————————— WHAT WILL YOU WRITE FOR THIS PROMPT? ————————————

———————————— WHAT KEY POINTS WILL YOU TALK ABOUT? ————————————

———————————— WHAT FORMAT WILL YOU USE? ————————————

POST   REEL   INFO GRAPHIC   LIVE/IGTV   STORY

HOW ARE YOU FEELING TODAY?

DID YOU MAKE ANY SALES TODAY?

HOW MANY PEOPLE DID YOU TALK TO?

WHO ARE THEY?

WHO IS A WARM LEAD TODAY?

WHAT ARE YOU GOING TO DO TOMORROW
TO MOVE YOU FORWARDS?

(FIRST) 30 DAY CYCLE

M T W T F S S / WEEK 1 2 3 4 5

1 2 3 4 5 6 7 8 9 10 11 12 13 14 15 16 17
18 19 20 21 22 23 24 25 26 27 28 29 30 31

YOU ARE IN **KNOW ME**, HERE'S A PROMPT:
What's your elevator pitch?

──────── WHAT WILL YOU WRITE FOR THIS PROMPT? ────────

──────── WHAT KEY POINTS WILL YOU TALK ABOUT? ────────

──────── WHAT FORMAT WILL YOU USE? ────────

POST   REEL   INFO GRAPHIC   LIVE/IGTV   STORY

HOW ARE YOU FEELING TODAY?

DID YOU MAKE ANY SALES TODAY?

HOW MANY PEOPLE DID YOU TALK TO?

WHO ARE THEY?

WHO IS A WARM LEAD TODAY?

WHAT ARE YOU GOING TO DO TOMORROW
TO MOVE YOU FORWARDS?

(FIRST) 30 DAY CYCLE

M T W T F S S / WEEK 1 2 3 4 5

1 2 3 4 5 6 7 8 9 10 11 12 13 14 15 16 17
18 19 20 21 22 23 24 25 26 27 28 29 30 31

_____

_____

_____

_____

YOU ARE IN **KNOW ME**, HERE'S A PROMPT:
What's an easy and relatable fact about you?

──────── WHAT WILL YOU WRITE FOR THIS PROMPT? ────────

──────── WHAT KEY POINTS WILL YOU TALK ABOUT? ────────

──────── WHAT FORMAT WILL YOU USE? ────────

POST   REEL   INFO GRAPHIC   LIVE/IGTV   STORY

HOW ARE YOU FEELING TODAY?

DID YOU MAKE ANY SALES TODAY?

HOW MANY PEOPLE DID YOU TALK TO?

WHO ARE THEY?

WHO IS A WARM LEAD TODAY?

WHAT ARE YOU GOING TO DO TOMORROW TO MAKE MORE SALES?

(FIRST) 30 DAY CYCLE

M T W T F S S / WEEK 1 2 3 4 5

1 2 3 4 5 6 7 8 9 10 11 12 13 14 15 16 17
18 19 20 21 22 23 24 25 26 27 28 29 30 31

_____

_____

_____

_____

_____

YOU ARE IN **KNOW ME**, HERE'S A PROMPT:
Why did you start your business?

———————— WHAT WILL YOU WRITE FOR THIS PROMPT? ————————

———————— WHAT KEY POINTS WILL YOU TALK ABOUT? ————————

———————— WHAT FORMAT WILL YOU USE? ————————

POST   REEL   INFO GRAPHIC   LIVE/IGTV   STORY

HOW ARE YOU FEELING TODAY?

DID YOU MAKE ANY SALES TODAY?

HOW MANY PEOPLE DID YOU TALK TO?

WHO ARE THEY?

WHO IS A WARM LEAD TODAY?

WHAT ARE YOU GOING TO DO TOMORROW
TO MOVE YOU FORWARDS?

FIRST 30 DAY CYCLE

M T W T F S S / WEEK 1 2 3 4 5

1 2 3 4 5 6 7 8 9 10 11 12 13 14 15 16 17
18 19 20 21 22 23 24 25 26 27 28 29 30 31

YOU ARE IN **KNOW ME**, HERE'S A PROMPT:
What helps you do your job?

──────── WHAT WILL YOU WRITE FOR THIS PROMPT? ────────

──────── WHAT KEY POINTS WILL YOU TALK ABOUT? ────────

──────── WHAT FORMAT WILL YOU USE? ────────

POST   REEL   INFO GRAPHIC   LIVE/IGTV   STORY

HOW ARE YOU FEELING TODAY?

😰 😕 🤔 😐 😊 😁

DID YOU MAKE ANY SALES TODAY?

HOW MANY PEOPLE DID YOU TALK TO?

WHO ARE THEY?

WHO IS A WARM LEAD TODAY?

WHAT ARE YOU GOING TO DO TOMORROW
TO MOVE YOU FORWARDS?

(FIRST) 30 DAY CYCLE

M T W T F S S   /   WEEK 1 2 3 4 5

1 2 3 4 5 6 7 8 9 10 11 12 13 14 15 16 17
18 19 20 21 22 23 24 25 26 27 28 29 30 31

_____

_____

_____

_____

YOU ARE IN **KNOW ME**, HERE'S A PROMPT:
The results that you or your products/service create for someone.

———————— WHAT WILL YOU WRITE FOR THIS PROMPT? ————————

———————— WHAT KEY POINTS WILL YOU TALK ABOUT? ————————

———————— WHAT FORMAT WILL YOU USE? ————————

POST   REEL   INFO GRAPHIC   LIVE/IGTV   STORY

DID YOU MAKE ANY SALES TODAY?

HOW MANY PEOPLE DID YOU TALK TO?

WHO ARE THEY?

WHO IS A WARM LEAD TODAY?

WHAT ARE YOU GOING TO DO TOMORROW
TO MAKE MORE SALES?

FIRST 30 DAY CYCLE

M T W T F S S / WEEK 1 2 3 4 5

1 2 3 4 5 6 7 8 9 10 11 12 13 14 15 16 17
18 19 20 21 22 23 24 25 26 27 28 29 30 31

YOU ARE IN **KNOW ME**, HERE'S A PROMPT:
Tell us a little bit about what your business does (for those of us who may have only just found you).

———————— WHAT WILL YOU WRITE FOR THIS PROMPT? ————————

———————— WHAT KEY POINTS WILL YOU TALK ABOUT? ————————

———————— WHAT FORMAT WILL YOU USE? ————————

POST   REEL   INFO GRAPHIC   LIVE/IGTV   STORY

HOW ARE YOU FEELING TODAY?

DID YOU MAKE ANY SALES TODAY?

HOW MANY PEOPLE DID YOU TALK TO?

WHO ARE THEY?

WHO IS A WARM LEAD TODAY?

WHAT ARE YOU GOING TO DO TOMORROW
TO MOVE YOU FORWARDS?

(FIRST) 30 DAY CYCLE

M T W T F S S / WEEK 1 2 3 4 5

1 2 3 4 5 6 7 8 9 10 11 12 13 14 15 16 17
18 19 20 21 22 23 24 25 26 27 28 29 30 31

YOU ARE IN **KNOW ME**, HERE'S A PROMPT:
A case study of your work.

──────── WHAT WILL YOU WRITE FOR THIS PROMPT? ────────

──────── WHAT KEY POINTS WILL YOU TALK ABOUT? ────────

──────── WHAT FORMAT WILL YOU USE? ────────

POST   REEL   INFO GRAPHIC   LIVE/IGTV   STORY

HOW ARE YOU FEELING TODAY?

DID YOU MAKE ANY SALES TODAY?

HOW MANY PEOPLE DID YOU TALK TO?

WHO ARE THEY?

WHO IS A WARM LEAD TODAY?

WHAT ARE YOU GOING TO DO TOMORROW
TO MOVE YOU FORWARDS?

(FIRST) 30 DAY CYCLE

M T W T F S S / WEEK 1 2 3 4 5

1 2 3 4 5 6 7 8 9 10 11 12 13 14 15 16 17
18 19 20 21 22 23 24 25 26 27 28 29 30 31

YOU ARE IN **KNOW ME**, HERE'S A PROMPT:
Problems you can fix with your business?

———————— WHAT WILL YOU WRITE FOR THIS PROMPT? ————————

———————— WHAT KEY POINTS WILL YOU TALK ABOUT? ————————

———————— WHAT FORMAT WILL YOU USE? ————————

POST   REEL   INFO GRAPHIC   LIVE/IGTV   STORY

HOW ARE YOU FEELING TODAY?

DID YOU MAKE ANY SALES TODAY?

HOW MANY PEOPLE DID YOU TALK TO?

WHO ARE THEY?

WHO IS A WARM LEAD TODAY?

WHAT ARE YOU GOING TO DO TOMORROW
TO MOVE YOU FORWARDS?

(FIRST) 30 DAY CYCLE

M T W T F S S / WEEK 1 2 3 4 5

1 2 3 4 5 6 7 8 9 10 11 12 13 14 15 16 17
18 19 20 21 22 23 24 25 26 27 28 29 30 31

_____

_____

_____

_____

YOU ARE IN **KNOW ME**, HERE'S A PROMPT:
What stands out to you in your industry?

──────── WHAT WILL YOU WRITE FOR THIS PROMPT? ────────

──────── WHAT KEY POINTS WILL YOU TALK ABOUT? ────────

──────── WHAT FORMAT WILL YOU USE? ────────

POST   REEL   INFO GRAPHIC   LIVE/IGTV   STORY

HOW ARE YOU FEELING TODAY?

DID YOU MAKE ANY SALES TODAY?

HOW MANY PEOPLE DID YOU TALK TO?

WHO ARE THEY?

WHO IS A WARM LEAD TODAY?

WHAT ARE YOU GOING TO DO TOMORROW TO MOVE YOU FORWARDS?

10 Day Check In, how's it going?

HOW IS YOUR CONTENT PERFORMING?

BEST PERFORMING CONTENT?

LEAST PERFORMING CONTENT?

REACH	PROFILE VISITS	NEW FOLLOWERS	CONTENT INTERACTIONS	WEBSITE TAPS
◯	◯	◯	◯	◯

HOW DO YOU FEEL THINGS ARE GOING?

FREEWRITE

(FIRST) 30 DAY CYCLE

M T W T F S S / WEEK 1 2 3 4 5

1 2 3 4 5 6 7 8 9 10 11 12 13 14 15 16 17
18 19 20 21 22 23 24 25 26 27 28 29 30 31

_____
_____
_____
_____

YOU ARE IN **KNOW ME**, HERE'S A PROMPT:
Why are you passionate about what you do?

———————— WHAT WILL YOU WRITE FOR THIS PROMPT? ————————

———————— WHAT KEY POINTS WILL YOU TALK ABOUT? ————————

———————— WHAT FORMAT WILL YOU USE? ————————

POST   REEL   INFO GRAPHIC   LIVE/IGTV   STORY

HOW ARE YOU FEELING TODAY?

DID YOU MAKE ANY SALES TODAY?

HOW MANY PEOPLE DID YOU TALK TO?

WHO ARE THEY?

WHO IS A WARM LEAD TODAY?

WHAT ARE YOU GOING TO DO TOMORROW
TO MOVE YOU FORWARDS?

$\left(\text{FIRST}\right)$ 30 DAY CYCLE

M T W T F S S / WEEK 1 2 3 4 5

1 2 3 4 5 6 7 8 9 10 11 12 13 14 15 16 17
18 19 20 21 22 23 24 25 26 27 28 29 30 31

YOU ARE IN **KNOW ME**, HERE'S A PROMPT:
What inspired you to start your business?

—————— WHAT WILL YOU WRITE FOR THIS PROMPT? ——————

—————— WHAT KEY POINTS WILL YOU TALK ABOUT? ——————

—————— WHAT FORMAT WILL YOU USE? ——————

POST   REEL   INFO GRAPHIC   LIVE/IGTV   STORY

HOW ARE YOU FEELING TODAY?

DID YOU MAKE ANY SALES TODAY?

HOW MANY PEOPLE DID YOU TALK TO?

WHO ARE THEY?

WHO IS A WARM LEAD TODAY?

WHAT ARE YOU GOING TO DO TOMORROW TO MOVE YOU FORWARDS?

(FIRST) 30 DAY CYCLE

M T W T F S S / WEEK 1 2 3 4 5

1 2 3 4 5 6 7 8 9 10 11 12 13 14 15 16 17
18 19 20 21 22 23 24 25 26 27 28 29 30 31

_____

_____

_____

_____

YOU ARE IN **KNOW ME**, HERE'S A PROMPT:
The benefits of your business for a follower?

———————— WHAT WILL YOU WRITE FOR THIS PROMPT? ————————

———————— WHAT KEY POINTS WILL YOU TALK ABOUT? ————————

———————— WHAT FORMAT WILL YOU USE? ————————

POST   REEL   INFO GRAPHIC   LIVE/IGTV   STORY

HOW ARE YOU FEELING TODAY?

DID YOU MAKE ANY SALES TODAY?

HOW MANY PEOPLE DID YOU TALK TO?

WHO ARE THEY?

WHO IS A WARM LEAD TODAY?

WHAT ARE YOU GOING TO DO TOMORROW
TO MOVE YOU FORWARDS?

 FIRST 30 DAY CYCLE

M T W T F S S / WEEK 1 2 3 4 5

1 2 3 4 5 6 7 8 9 10 11 12 13 14 15 16 17
18 19 20 21 22 23 24 25 26 27 28 29 30 31

YOU ARE IN **KNOW ME**, HERE'S A PROMPT:
Which public figure do you like and why do they inspire you?

──────── WHAT WILL YOU WRITE FOR THIS PROMPT? ────────

──────── WHAT KEY POINTS WILL YOU TALK ABOUT? ────────

──────── WHAT FORMAT WILL YOU USE? ────────

POST   REEL   INFO GRAPHIC   LIVE/IGTV   STORY

HOW ARE YOU FEELING TODAY?

DID YOU MAKE ANY SALES TODAY?

HOW MANY PEOPLE DID YOU TALK TO?

WHO ARE THEY?

WHO IS A WARM LEAD TODAY?

WHAT ARE YOU GOING TO DO TOMORROW TO MOVE YOU FORWARDS?

(FIRST) 30 DAY CYCLE

M T W T F S S / WEEK 1 2 3 4 5

1 2 3 4 5 6 7 8 9 10 11 12 13 14 15 16 17
18 19 20 21 22 23 24 25 26 27 28 29 30 31

YOU ARE IN **KNOW ME**, HERE'S A PROMPT:
Tell us about yourself and your role in your business?

──────────── WHAT WILL YOU WRITE FOR THIS PROMPT? ────────────

──────────── WHAT KEY POINTS WILL YOU TALK ABOUT? ────────────

──────────── WHAT FORMAT WILL YOU USE? ────────────

POST   REEL   INFO GRAPHIC   LIVE/IGTV   STORY

HOW ARE YOU FEELING TODAY?

DID YOU MAKE ANY SALES TODAY?

HOW MANY PEOPLE DID YOU TALK TO?

WHO ARE THEY?

WHO IS A WARM LEAD TODAY?

WHAT ARE YOU GOING TO DO TOMORROW
TO MOVE YOU FORWARDS?

(FIRST) 30 DAY CYCLE

M T W T F S S / WEEK 1 2 3 4 5
1 2 3 4 5 6 7 8 9 10 11 12 13 14 15 16 17
18 19 20 21 22 23 24 25 26 27 28 29 30 31

YOU ARE IN **KNOW ME**, HERE'S A PROMPT:
Share a helpful tip.

──────── WHAT WILL YOU WRITE FOR THIS PROMPT? ────────

──────── WHAT KEY POINTS WILL YOU TALK ABOUT? ────────

──────── WHAT FORMAT WILL YOU USE? ────────

POST   REEL   INFO GRAPHIC   LIVE/IGTV   STORY

HOW ARE YOU FEELING TODAY?

DID YOU MAKE ANY SALES TODAY?

HOW MANY PEOPLE DID YOU TALK TO?

WHO ARE THEY?

WHO IS A WARM LEAD TODAY?

WHAT ARE YOU GOING TO DO TOMORROW TO MOVE YOU FORWARDS?

(FIRST) 30 DAY CYCLE

M T W T F S S / WEEK 1 2 3 4 5

1 2 3 4 5 6 7 8 9 10 11 12 13 14 15 16 17
18 19 20 21 22 23 24 25 26 27 28 29 30 31

_____

_____

_____

_____

YOU ARE IN **KNOW ME**, HERE'S A PROMPT:
What emotion do you want people to feel after they've worked with you?

──────────── WHAT WILL YOU WRITE FOR THIS PROMPT? ────────────

──────────── WHAT KEY POINTS WILL YOU TALK ABOUT? ────────────

──────────── WHAT FORMAT WILL YOU USE? ────────────

POST   REEL   INFO GRAPHIC   LIVE/IGTV   STORY

HOW ARE YOU FEELING TODAY?

DID YOU MAKE ANY SALES TODAY?

HOW MANY PEOPLE DID YOU TALK TO?

WHO ARE THEY?

WHO IS A WARM LEAD TODAY?

WHAT ARE YOU GOING TO DO TOMORROW
TO MOVE YOU FORWARDS?

(FIRST) 30 DAY CYCLE

M T W T F S S / WEEK 1 2 3 4 5

1 2 3 4 5 6 7 8 9 10 11 12 13 14 15 16 17
18 19 20 21 22 23 24 25 26 27 28 29 30 31

YOU ARE IN **KNOW ME**, HERE'S A PROMPT:
What personality trait of yours helps you in business?

─────── WHAT WILL YOU WRITE FOR THIS PROMPT? ───────

─────── WHAT KEY POINTS WILL YOU TALK ABOUT? ───────

─────── WHAT FORMAT WILL YOU USE? ───────

POST   REEL   INFO GRAPHIC   LIVE/IGTV   STORY

HOW ARE YOU FEELING TODAY?

DID YOU MAKE ANY SALES TODAY?

HOW MANY PEOPLE DID YOU TALK TO?

WHO ARE THEY?

WHO IS A WARM LEAD TODAY?

WHAT ARE YOU GOING TO DO TOMORROW
TO MOVE YOU FORWARDS?

(FIRST) 30 DAY CYCLE

M T W T F S S / WEEK 1 2 3 4 5

1 2 3 4 5 6 7 8 9 10 11 12 13 14 15 16 17
18 19 20 21 22 23 24 25 26 27 28 29 30 31

_____

_____

_____

_____

YOU ARE IN **KNOW ME**, HERE'S A PROMPT:
Why do you do what you do beyond making money and it being a job?

———————— WHAT WILL YOU WRITE FOR THIS PROMPT? ————————

———————— WHAT KEY POINTS WILL YOU TALK ABOUT? ————————

———————— WHAT FORMAT WILL YOU USE? ————————

POST   REEL   INFO GRAPHIC   LIVE/IGTV   STORY

HOW ARE YOU FEELING TODAY?

DID YOU MAKE ANY SALES TODAY?

HOW MANY PEOPLE DID YOU TALK TO?

WHO ARE THEY?

WHO IS A WARM LEAD TODAY?

WHAT ARE YOU GOING TO DO TOMORROW
TO MOVE YOU FORWARDS?

(FIRST) 30 DAY CYCLE

M T W T F S S / WEEK 1 2 3 4 5

1 2 3 4 5 6 7 8 9 10 11 12 13 14 15 16 17
18 19 20 21 22 23 24 25 26 27 28 29 30 31

_____

_____

_____

_____

YOU ARE IN **LIKE ME**, HERE'S A PROMPT:
*What's the best piece of advice you could give
your customers/clients?*

──────── WHAT WILL YOU WRITE FOR THIS PROMPT? ────────

──────── WHAT KEY POINTS WILL YOU TALK ABOUT? ────────

──────── WHAT FORMAT WILL YOU USE? ────────

POST   REEL   INFO GRAPHIC   LIVE/IGTV   STORY

HOW ARE YOU FEELING TODAY?

DID YOU MAKE ANY SALES TODAY?

HOW MANY PEOPLE DID YOU TALK TO?

WHO ARE THEY?

WHO IS A WARM LEAD TODAY?

WHAT ARE YOU GOING TO DO TOMORROW
TO MOVE YOU FORWARDS?

10 Day Check In, how's it going?

HOW IS YOUR CONTENT PERFORMING?

BEST PERFORMING CONTENT?

LEAST PERFORMING CONTENT?

REACH	PROFILE VISITS	NEW FOLLOWERS	CONTENT INTERACTIONS	WEBSITE TAPS
◯	◯	◯	◯	◯

HOW DO YOU FEEL THINGS ARE GOING?

FREEWRITE

 FIRST 30 DAY CYCLE

M T W T F S S / WEEK 1 2 3 4 5

1 2 3 4 5 6 7 8 9 10 11 12 13 14 15 16 17
18 19 20 21 22 23 24 25 26 27 28 29 30 31

YOU ARE IN **LIKE ME**, HERE'S A PROMPT:
What problems do you love to solve?

———————— WHAT WILL YOU WRITE FOR THIS PROMPT? ————————

———————— WHAT KEY POINTS WILL YOU TALK ABOUT? ————————

———————— WHAT FORMAT WILL YOU USE? ————————

POST   REEL   INFO GRAPHIC   LIVE/IGTV   STORY

HOW ARE YOU FEELING TODAY?

DID YOU MAKE ANY SALES TODAY?

HOW MANY PEOPLE DID YOU TALK TO?

WHO ARE THEY?

WHO IS A WARM LEAD TODAY?

WHAT ARE YOU GOING TO DO TOMORROW
TO MOVE YOU FORWARDS?

(FIRST) 30 DAY CYCLE

M T W T F S S / WEEK 1 2 3 4 5

1 2 3 4 5 6 7 8 9 10 11 12 13 14 15 16 17
18 19 20 21 22 23 24 25 26 27 28 29 30 31

_____
_____
_____
_____

YOU ARE IN **LIKE ME**, HERE'S A PROMPT:
Who was your last customer?

——————— WHAT WILL YOU WRITE FOR THIS PROMPT? ———————

——————— WHAT KEY POINTS WILL YOU TALK ABOUT? ———————

——————— WHAT FORMAT WILL YOU USE? ———————

POST   REEL   INFO GRAPHIC   LIVE/IGTV   STORY

HOW ARE YOU FEELING TODAY?

DID YOU MAKE ANY SALES TODAY?

HOW MANY PEOPLE DID YOU TALK TO?

WHO ARE THEY?

WHO IS A WARM LEAD TODAY?

WHAT ARE YOU GOING TO DO TOMORROW
TO MOVE YOU FORWARDS?

(FIRST) 30 DAY CYCLE

M T W T F S S / WEEK 1 2 3 4 5

1 2 3 4 5 6 7 8 9 10 11 12 13 14 15 16 17
18 19 20 21 22 23 24 25 26 27 28 29 30 31

YOU ARE IN **LIKE ME**, HERE'S A PROMPT:
How long have you been in business or training for your business?

——————— WHAT WILL YOU WRITE FOR THIS PROMPT? ———————

——————— WHAT KEY POINTS WILL YOU TALK ABOUT? ———————

——————— WHAT FORMAT WILL YOU USE? ———————

POST   REEL   INFO GRAPHIC   LIVE/IGTV   STORY

HOW ARE YOU FEELING TODAY?

DID YOU MAKE ANY SALES TODAY?

HOW MANY PEOPLE DID YOU TALK TO?

WHO ARE THEY?

WHO IS A WARM LEAD TODAY?

WHAT ARE YOU GOING TO DO TOMORROW
TO MOVE YOU FORWARDS?

$\left(\text{FIRST}\right)$ 30 DAY CYCLE

M T W T F S S / WEEK 1 2 3 4 5

1 2 3 4 5 6 7 8 9 10 11 12 13 14 15 16 17
18 19 20 21 22 23 24 25 26 27 28 29 30 31

YOU ARE IN **LIKE ME**, HERE'S A PROMPT:
Something about you that people can relate to that is very normal to your ideal client.

———————— WHAT WILL YOU WRITE FOR THIS PROMPT? ————————

———————— WHAT KEY POINTS WILL YOU TALK ABOUT? ————————

———————— WHAT FORMAT WILL YOU USE? ————————

POST   REEL   INFO GRAPHIC   LIVE/IGTV   STORY

──────── HOW ARE YOU FEELING TODAY? ────────

😰 😟 😕 😐 😊 😄

──────── DID YOU MAKE ANY SALES TODAY? ────────

──────── HOW MANY PEOPLE DID YOU TALK TO? ────────

──────── WHO ARE THEY? ────────

──────── WHO IS A WARM LEAD TODAY? ────────

──────── WHAT ARE YOU GOING TO DO TOMORROW
TO MOVE YOU FORWARDS? ────────

(FIRST) 30 DAY CYCLE

M T W T F S S / WEEK 1 2 3 4 5

1 2 3 4 5 6 7 8 9 10 11 12 13 14 15 16 17
18 19 20 21 22 23 24 25 26 27 28 29 30 31

_____

_____

_____

_____

YOU ARE IN **LIKE ME**, HERE'S A PROMPT:
A fun fact about your service or product?

——————— WHAT WILL YOU WRITE FOR THIS PROMPT? ———————

——————— WHAT KEY POINTS WILL YOU TALK ABOUT? ———————

——————— WHAT FORMAT WILL YOU USE? ———————

POST   REEL   INFO GRAPHIC   LIVE/IGTV   STORY

HOW ARE YOU FEELING TODAY?

DID YOU MAKE ANY SALES TODAY?

HOW MANY PEOPLE DID YOU TALK TO?

WHO ARE THEY?

WHO IS A WARM LEAD TODAY?

WHAT ARE YOU GOING TO DO TOMORROW
TO MOVE YOU FORWARDS?

$\widehat{\text{FIRST}}$ 30 DAY CYCLE

M T W T F S S / WEEK 1 2 3 4 5

1 2 3 4 5 6 7 8 9 10 11 12 13 14 15 16 17
18 19 20 21 22 23 24 25 26 27 28 29 30 31

YOU ARE IN **LIKE ME**, HERE'S A PROMPT:
The benefits of you as the business owner.

──────── WHAT WILL YOU WRITE FOR THIS PROMPT? ────────

──────── WHAT KEY POINTS WILL YOU TALK ABOUT? ────────

──────── WHAT FORMAT WILL YOU USE? ────────

POST   REEL   INFO GRAPHIC   LIVE/IGTV   STORY

HOW ARE YOU FEELING TODAY?

DID YOU MAKE ANY SALES TODAY?

HOW MANY PEOPLE DID YOU TALK TO?

WHO ARE THEY?

WHO IS A WARM LEAD TODAY?

WHAT ARE YOU GOING TO DO TOMORROW
TO MOVE YOU FORWARDS?

(FIRST) 30 DAY CYCLE

M T W T F S S / WEEK 1 2 3 4 5

1 2 3 4 5 6 7 8 9 10 11 12 13 14 15 16 17
18 19 20 21 22 23 24 25 26 27 28 29 30 31

_____

_____

_____

_____

YOU ARE IN **LIKE ME**, HERE'S A PROMPT:
What makes you light up?

──────── WHAT WILL YOU WRITE FOR THIS PROMPT? ────────

──────── WHAT KEY POINTS WILL YOU TALK ABOUT? ────────

──────── WHAT FORMAT WILL YOU USE? ────────

POST   REEL   INFO GRAPHIC   LIVE/IGTV   STORY

HOW ARE YOU FEELING TODAY?

DID YOU MAKE ANY SALES TODAY?

HOW MANY PEOPLE DID YOU TALK TO?

WHO ARE THEY?

WHO IS A WARM LEAD TODAY?

WHAT ARE YOU GOING TO DO TOMORROW TO MOVE YOU FORWARDS?

(FIRST) 30 DAY CYCLE

M T W T F S S / WEEK 1 2 3 4 5

1 2 3 4 5 6 7 8 9 10 11 12 13 14 15 16 17
18 19 20 21 22 23 24 25 26 27 28 29 30 31

_____

_____

_____

_____

YOU ARE IN **LIKE ME**, HERE'S A PROMPT:

Inspirational quote, can be in the photo or caption but one that your clients would like - not you.

———————— WHAT WILL YOU WRITE FOR THIS PROMPT? ————————

———————— WHAT KEY POINTS WILL YOU TALK ABOUT? ————————

———————— WHAT FORMAT WILL YOU USE? ————————

POST   REEL   INFO GRAPHIC   LIVE/IGTV   STORY

HOW ARE YOU FEELING TODAY?

DID YOU MAKE ANY SALES TODAY?

HOW MANY PEOPLE DID YOU TALK TO?

WHO ARE THEY?

WHO IS A WARM LEAD TODAY?

WHAT ARE YOU GOING TO DO TOMORROW
TO MOVE YOU FORWARDS?

$\left(\text{FIRST}\right)$30 DAY CYCLE

M T W T F S S / WEEK 1 2 3 4 5

1 2 3 4 5 6 7 8 9 10 11 12 13 14 15 16 17
18 19 20 21 22 23 24 25 26 27 28 29 30 31

YOU ARE IN **LIKE ME**, HERE'S A PROMPT:
Why did you create your signature service/source of your favourite product?

——————— WHAT WILL YOU WRITE FOR THIS PROMPT? ———————

——————— WHAT KEY POINTS WILL YOU TALK ABOUT? ———————

——————— WHAT FORMAT WILL YOU USE? ———————

POST   REEL   INFO GRAPHIC   LIVE/IGTV   STORY

HOW ARE YOU FEELING TODAY?

DID YOU MAKE ANY SALES TODAY?

HOW MANY PEOPLE DID YOU TALK TO?

WHO ARE THEY?

WHO IS A WARM LEAD TODAY?

WHAT ARE YOU GOING TO DO TOMORROW
TO MOVE YOU FORWARDS?

10 Day Check In, how's it going?

HOW IS YOUR CONTENT PERFORMING?

BEST PERFORMING CONTENT?

LEAST PERFORMING CONTENT?

REACH	PROFILE VISITS	NEW FOLLOWERS	CONTENT INTERACTIONS	WEBSITE TAPS
◯	◯	◯	◯	◯

HOW DO YOU FEEL THINGS ARE GOING?

FREEWRITE

End of Your First 30 Day Goal...

HOW MANY POSTS DID YOU DO?

○

HOW MANY PEOPLE DID YOU CONNECT WITH
THAT WILL HELP YOUR BUSINESS?

○

HOW MANY DAYS A WEEK DID
YOU POST STORIES?

○

HOW MUCH TIME DID YOU SPEND
INTERACTING, NOT BROWSING?

WHAT PERCENTAGE GROWTH DID
YOU ACHIEVE THIS MONTH?

○

1ST 30 DAY CYCLE - END OF CYCLE

HOW DID YOU FEEL ABOUT
INSTAGRAM THIS MONTH?

DO YOU NEED TO MUTE ANYONE?

FREEWRITE...

Onto the next
30 days...

Start Your Second 30 Day Goal

M T W T F S S / WEEK 1 2 3 4 5

JAN   FEB   MAR   APR   MAY   JUN   JUL   AUG   SEP   OCT   NOV   DEC

M   T   W   T   F   S   S

WRITE YOUR GOAL HERE

HOW MANY POSTS DO YOU
WANT TO MAKE A WEEK?

HOW MANY PEOPLE DO YOU WANT TO CONNECT
WITH THAT WILL HELP YOUR BUSINESS?

HOW MANY DAYS A WEEK DO
YOU PLAN TO POST STORIES?

HOW MUCH TIME WILL YOU SPEND INTERACTING, NOT BROWSING?

WHAT PERCENTAGE GROWTH ARE YOU HOPING TO ACHIEVE THIS MONTH?

ANY OTHER GOALS?

FREEWRITE...

SECOND 30 DAY CYCLE

M T W T F S S / WEEK 1 2 3 4 5

1 2 3 4 5 6 7 8 9 10 11 12 13 14 15 16 17
18 19 20 21 22 23 24 25 26 27 28 29 30 31

YOU ARE IN **LIKE ME**, HERE'S A PROMPT:
Talk about your plans for the week or what you've achieved this week.

———— WHAT WILL YOU WRITE FOR THIS PROMPT? ————

———— WHAT KEY POINTS WILL YOU TALK ABOUT? ————

———— WHAT FORMAT WILL YOU USE? ————

POST   REEL   INFO GRAPHIC   LIVE/IGTV   STORY

HOW ARE YOU FEELING TODAY?

DID YOU MAKE ANY SALES TODAY?

HOW MANY PEOPLE DID YOU TALK TO?

WHO ARE THEY?

WHO IS A WARM LEAD TODAY?

WHAT ARE YOU GOING TO DO TOMORROW
TO MOVE YOU FORWARDS?

 SECOND 30 DAY CYCLE

M T W T F S S / WEEK 1 2 3 4 5

1 2 3 4 5 6 7 8 9 10 11 12 13 14 15 16 17
18 19 20 21 22 23 24 25 26 27 28 29 30 31

_____

_____

_____

_____

YOU ARE IN **LIKE ME**, HERE'S A PROMPT:
Is your business location specific?

——————— WHAT WILL YOU WRITE FOR THIS PROMPT? ———————

——————— WHAT KEY POINTS WILL YOU TALK ABOUT? ———————

——————— WHAT FORMAT WILL YOU USE? ———————

POST   REEL   INFO GRAPHIC   LIVE/IGTV   STORY

HOW ARE YOU FEELING TODAY?

DID YOU MAKE ANY SALES TODAY?

HOW MANY PEOPLE DID YOU TALK TO?

WHO ARE THEY?

WHO IS A WARM LEAD TODAY?

WHAT ARE YOU GOING TO DO TOMORROW TO MOVE YOU FORWARDS?

(SECOND) 30 DAY CYCLE

M T W T F S S / WEEK 1 2 3 4 5

1 2 3 4 5 6 7 8 9 10 11 12 13 14 15 16 17
18 19 20 21 22 23 24 25 26 27 28 29 30 31

_____

_____

_____

_____

YOU ARE IN **LIKE ME**, HERE'S A PROMPT:
*When you could've done anything in the world,
why did you choose your business?*

———————— WHAT WILL YOU WRITE FOR THIS PROMPT? ————————

———————— WHAT KEY POINTS WILL YOU TALK ABOUT? ————————

———————— WHAT FORMAT WILL YOU USE? ————————

POST   REEL   INFO GRAPHIC   LIVE/IGTV   STORY

HOW ARE YOU FEELING TODAY?

DID YOU MAKE ANY SALES TODAY?

HOW MANY PEOPLE DID YOU TALK TO?

WHO ARE THEY?

WHO IS A WARM LEAD TODAY?

WHAT ARE YOU GOING TO DO TOMORROW
TO MOVE YOU FORWARDS?

SECOND 30 DAY CYCLE

M T W T F S S / WEEK 1 2 3 4 5

1 2 3 4 5 6 7 8 9 10 11 12 13 14 15 16 17
18 19 20 21 22 23 24 25 26 27 28 29 30 31

YOU ARE IN **LIKE ME**, HERE'S A PROMPT:
Controversial statement that goes against your industry but your client would agree with.

——— WHAT WILL YOU WRITE FOR THIS PROMPT? ———

——— WHAT KEY POINTS WILL YOU TALK ABOUT? ———

——— WHAT FORMAT WILL YOU USE? ———

POST   REEL   INFO GRAPHIC   LIVE/IGTV   STORY

HOW ARE YOU FEELING TODAY?

DID YOU MAKE ANY SALES TODAY?

HOW MANY PEOPLE DID YOU TALK TO?

WHO ARE THEY?

WHO IS A WARM LEAD TODAY?

WHAT ARE YOU GOING TO DO TOMORROW TO MOVE YOU FORWARDS?

$\left(\text{SECOND}\right)$ 30 DAY CYCLE

M T W T F S S / WEEK 1 2 3 4 5

1 2 3 4 5 6 7 8 9 10 11 12 13 14 15 16 17
18 19 20 21 22 23 24 25 26 27 28 29 30 31

_____

_____

_____

_____

YOU ARE IN **LIKE ME**, HERE'S A PROMPT:
Talk about the end product/ end dream of using your business for a customer.

———————— WHAT WILL YOU WRITE FOR THIS PROMPT? ————————

———————— WHAT KEY POINTS WILL YOU TALK ABOUT? ————————

———————— WHAT FORMAT WILL YOU USE? ————————

POST   REEL   INFO GRAPHIC   LIVE/IGTV   STORY

HOW ARE YOU FEELING TODAY?

DID YOU MAKE ANY SALES TODAY?

HOW MANY PEOPLE DID YOU TALK TO?

WHO ARE THEY?

WHO IS A WARM LEAD TODAY?

WHAT ARE YOU GOING TO DO TOMORROW TO MOVE YOU FORWARDS?

SECOND 30 DAY CYCLE

M T W T F S S / WEEK 1 2 3 4 5

1 2 3 4 5 6 7 8 9 10 11 12 13 14 15 16 17
18 19 20 21 22 23 24 25 26 27 28 29 30 31

YOU ARE IN **LIKE ME**, HERE'S A PROMPT:
Why you do what you do?

──────── WHAT WILL YOU WRITE FOR THIS PROMPT? ────────

──────── WHAT KEY POINTS WILL YOU TALK ABOUT? ────────

──────── WHAT FORMAT WILL YOU USE? ────────

POST   REEL   INFO GRAPHIC   LIVE/IGTV   STORY

HOW ARE YOU FEELING TODAY?

DID YOU MAKE ANY SALES TODAY?

HOW MANY PEOPLE DID YOU TALK TO?

WHO ARE THEY?

WHO IS A WARM LEAD TODAY?

WHAT ARE YOU GOING TO DO TOMORROW
TO MOVE YOU FORWARDS?

(SECOND) 30 DAY CYCLE

M T W T F S S / WEEK 1 2 3 4 5

1 2 3 4 5 6 7 8 9 10 11 12 13 14 15 16 17
18 19 20 21 22 23 24 25 26 27 28 29 30 31

_____
_____
_____
_____

YOU ARE IN **LIKE ME**, HERE'S A PROMPT:
What drives you to go even when you don't feel like it?

———————— WHAT WILL YOU WRITE FOR THIS PROMPT? ————————

———————— WHAT KEY POINTS WILL YOU TALK ABOUT? ————————

———————— WHAT FORMAT WILL YOU USE? ————————

POST   REEL   INFO GRAPHIC   LIVE/IGTV   STORY

HOW ARE YOU FEELING TODAY?

DID YOU MAKE ANY SALES TODAY?

HOW MANY PEOPLE DID YOU TALK TO?

WHO ARE THEY?

WHO IS A WARM LEAD TODAY?

WHAT ARE YOU GOING TO DO TOMORROW
TO MOVE YOU FORWARDS?

(SECOND) 30 DAY CYCLE

M T W T F S S / WEEK 1 2 3 4 5
1 2 3 4 5 6 7 8 9 10 11 12 13 14 15 16 17
18 19 20 21 22 23 24 25 26 27 28 29 30 31

YOU ARE IN **LIKE ME**, HERE'S A PROMPT:
Discuss a FAQ.

——————— WHAT WILL YOU WRITE FOR THIS PROMPT? ———————

——————— WHAT KEY POINTS WILL YOU TALK ABOUT? ———————

——————— WHAT FORMAT WILL YOU USE? ———————

POST   REEL   INFO GRAPHIC   LIVE/IGTV   STORY

HOW ARE YOU FEELING TODAY?

DID YOU MAKE ANY SALES TODAY?

HOW MANY PEOPLE DID YOU TALK TO?

WHO ARE THEY?

WHO IS A WARM LEAD TODAY?

WHAT ARE YOU GOING TO DO TOMORROW
TO MOVE YOU FORWARDS?

(SECOND) 30 DAY CYCLE

M T W T F S S / WEEK 1 2 3 4 5

1 2 3 4 5 6 7 8 9 10 11 12 13 14 15 16 17
18 19 20 21 22 23 24 25 26 27 28 29 30 31

_____

_____

_____

_____

_____

YOU ARE IN **LIKE ME**, HERE'S A PROMPT:
Talk about a recent article you read and discuss the points of it.

———————— WHAT WILL YOU WRITE FOR THIS PROMPT? ————————

———————— WHAT KEY POINTS WILL YOU TALK ABOUT? ————————

———————— WHAT FORMAT WILL YOU USE? ————————

POST   REEL   INFO GRAPHIC   LIVE/IGTV   STORY

HOW ARE YOU FEELING TODAY?

DID YOU MAKE ANY SALES TODAY?

HOW MANY PEOPLE DID YOU TALK TO?

WHO ARE THEY?

WHO IS A WARM LEAD TODAY?

WHAT ARE YOU GOING TO DO TOMORROW
TO MOVE YOU FORWARDS?

(SECOND) 30 DAY CYCLE

M T W T F S S / WEEK 1 2 3 4 5

1 2 3 4 5 6 7 8 9 10 11 12 13 14 15 16 17
18 19 20 21 22 23 24 25 26 27 28 29 30 31

_____
_____
_____
_____

YOU ARE IN **LIKE ME**, HERE'S A PROMPT:
What is your ideal client like?

———— WHAT WILL YOU WRITE FOR THIS PROMPT? ————

———— WHAT KEY POINTS WILL YOU TALK ABOUT? ————

———— WHAT FORMAT WILL YOU USE? ————

POST   REEL   INFO GRAPHIC   LIVE/IGTV   STORY

HOW ARE YOU FEELING TODAY?

DID YOU MAKE ANY SALES TODAY?

HOW MANY PEOPLE DID YOU TALK TO?

WHO ARE THEY?

WHO IS A WARM LEAD TODAY?

WHAT ARE YOU GOING TO DO TOMORROW
TO MOVE YOU FORWARDS?

10 Day Check In, how's it going?

HOW IS YOUR CONTENT PERFORMING?

BEST PERFORMING CONTENT?

LEAST PERFORMING CONTENT?

REACH	PROFILE VISITS	NEW FOLLOWERS	CONTENT INTERACTIONS	WEBSITE TAPS
◯	◯	◯	◯	◯

HOW DO YOU FEEL THINGS ARE GOING?

FREEWRITE

$\big(\text{SECOND}\big)$ 30 DAY CYCLE

M T W T F S S / WEEK 1 2 3 4 5

1 2 3 4 5 6 7 8 9 10 11 12 13 14 15 16 17
18 19 20 21 22 23 24 25 26 27 28 29 30 31

YOU ARE IN **TRUST ME**, HERE'S A PROMPT:
A peer review from someone in your business circle.

———————— WHAT WILL YOU WRITE FOR THIS PROMPT? ————————

———————— WHAT KEY POINTS WILL YOU TALK ABOUT? ————————

———————— WHAT FORMAT WILL YOU USE? ————————

POST   REEL   INFO GRAPHIC   LIVE/IGTV   STORY

HOW ARE YOU FEELING TODAY?

DID YOU MAKE ANY SALES TODAY?

HOW MANY PEOPLE DID YOU TALK TO?

WHO ARE THEY?

WHO IS A WARM LEAD TODAY?

WHAT ARE YOU GOING TO DO TOMORROW TO MOVE YOU FORWARDS?

SECOND 30 DAY CYCLE

M T W T F S S / WEEK 1 2 3 4 5
1 2 3 4 5 6 7 8 9 10 11 12 13 14 15 16 17
18 19 20 21 22 23 24 25 26 27 28 29 30 31

_____

_____

_____

_____

YOU ARE IN **TRUST ME**, HERE'S A PROMPT:
Do you ever turn people down/ turn away customers or clients?

──────── WHAT WILL YOU WRITE FOR THIS PROMPT? ────────

──────── WHAT KEY POINTS WILL YOU TALK ABOUT? ────────

──────── WHAT FORMAT WILL YOU USE? ────────

POST   REEL   INFO GRAPHIC   LIVE/IGTV   STORY

HOW ARE YOU FEELING TODAY?

DID YOU MAKE ANY SALES TODAY?

HOW MANY PEOPLE DID YOU TALK TO?

WHO ARE THEY?

WHO IS A WARM LEAD TODAY?

WHAT ARE YOU GOING TO DO TOMORROW
TO MOVE YOU FORWARDS?

SECOND 30 DAY CYCLE

M T W T F S S / WEEK 1 2 3 4 5

1 2 3 4 5 6 7 8 9 10 11 12 13 14 15 16 17
18 19 20 21 22 23 24 25 26 27 28 29 30 31

YOU ARE IN **TRUST ME**, HERE'S A PROMPT:
What's your story why are you in business?

———— WHAT WILL YOU WRITE FOR THIS PROMPT? ————

———— WHAT KEY POINTS WILL YOU TALK ABOUT? ————

———— WHAT FORMAT WILL YOU USE? ————

POST   REEL   INFO GRAPHIC   LIVE/IGTV   STORY

HOW ARE YOU FEELING TODAY?

DID YOU MAKE ANY SALES TODAY?

HOW MANY PEOPLE DID YOU TALK TO?

WHO ARE THEY?

WHO IS A WARM LEAD TODAY?

WHAT ARE YOU GOING TO DO TOMORROW
TO MOVE YOU FORWARDS?

(SECOND) 30 DAY CYCLE

M	T	W	T	F	S	S	/	WEEK	1	2	3	4	5

1 2 3 4 5 6 7 8 9 10 11 12 13 14 15 16 17
18 19 20 21 22 23 24 25 26 27 28 29 30 31

YOU ARE IN **TRUST ME**, HERE'S A PROMPT:
Talk about one of your services/products and describe it.

──────── WHAT WILL YOU WRITE FOR THIS PROMPT? ────────

──────── WHAT KEY POINTS WILL YOU TALK ABOUT? ────────

──────── WHAT FORMAT WILL YOU USE? ────────

POST   REEL   INFO GRAPHIC   LIVE/IGTV   STORY

HOW ARE YOU FEELING TODAY?

DID YOU MAKE ANY SALES TODAY?

HOW MANY PEOPLE DID YOU TALK TO?

WHO ARE THEY?

WHO IS A WARM LEAD TODAY?

WHAT ARE YOU GOING TO DO TOMORROW
TO MOVE YOU FORWARDS?

 SECOND 30 DAY CYCLE

M T W T F S S / WEEK 1 2 3 4 5

1 2 3 4 5 6 7 8 9 10 11 12 13 14 15 16 17
18 19 20 21 22 23 24 25 26 27 28 29 30 31

YOU ARE IN **TRUST ME**, HERE'S A PROMPT:
What do you change in people?

———————— WHAT WILL YOU WRITE FOR THIS PROMPT? ————————

———————— WHAT KEY POINTS WILL YOU TALK ABOUT? ————————

———————— WHAT FORMAT WILL YOU USE? ————————

POST   REEL   INFO GRAPHIC   LIVE/IGTV   STORY

HOW ARE YOU FEELING TODAY?

DID YOU MAKE ANY SALES TODAY?

HOW MANY PEOPLE DID YOU TALK TO?

WHO ARE THEY?

WHO IS A WARM LEAD TODAY?

WHAT ARE YOU GOING TO DO TOMORROW TO MOVE YOU FORWARDS?

 SECOND 30 DAY CYCLE

M T W T F S S / WEEK 1 2 3 4 5

1 2 3 4 5 6 7 8 9 10 11 12 13 14 15 16 17
18 19 20 21 22 23 24 25 26 27 28 29 30 31

_____

_____

_____

_____

YOU ARE IN **TRUST ME**, HERE'S A PROMPT:
Describe a recent testimonial how you received it.

———————— WHAT WILL YOU WRITE FOR THIS PROMPT? ————————

———————— WHAT KEY POINTS WILL YOU TALK ABOUT? ————————

———————— WHAT FORMAT WILL YOU USE? ————————

POST   REEL   INFO GRAPHIC   LIVE/IGTV   STORY

HOW ARE YOU FEELING TODAY?

DID YOU MAKE ANY SALES TODAY?

HOW MANY PEOPLE DID YOU TALK TO?

WHO ARE THEY?

WHO IS A WARM LEAD TODAY?

WHAT ARE YOU GOING TO DO TOMORROW
TO MOVE YOU FORWARDS?

(SECOND) 30 DAY CYCLE

M T W T F S S / WEEK 1 2 3 4 5

1 2 3 4 5 6 7 8 9 10 11 12 13 14 15 16 17
18 19 20 21 22 23 24 25 26 27 28 29 30 31

_____

_____

_____

_____

_____

YOU ARE IN **TRUST ME**, HERE'S A PROMPT:
Share something inspirational.

———————— WHAT WILL YOU WRITE FOR THIS PROMPT? ————————

———————— WHAT KEY POINTS WILL YOU TALK ABOUT? ————————

———————— WHAT FORMAT WILL YOU USE? ————————

POST   REEL   INFO GRAPHIC   LIVE/IGTV   STORY

HOW ARE YOU FEELING TODAY?

DID YOU MAKE ANY SALES TODAY?

HOW MANY PEOPLE DID YOU TALK TO?

WHO ARE THEY?

WHO IS A WARM LEAD TODAY?

WHAT ARE YOU GOING TO DO TOMORROW TO MOVE YOU FORWARDS?

(SECOND) 30 DAY CYCLE

M T W T F S S / WEEK 1 2 3 4 5

1 2 3 4 5 6 7 8 9 10 11 12 13 14 15 16 17
18 19 20 21 22 23 24 25 26 27 28 29 30 31

YOU ARE IN **TRUST ME**, HERE'S A PROMPT:
Have you trained for your business or do you have any relevant life experience?

———————————— WHAT WILL YOU WRITE FOR THIS PROMPT? ————————————

———————————— WHAT KEY POINTS WILL YOU TALK ABOUT? ————————————

———————————— WHAT FORMAT WILL YOU USE? ————————————

POST   REEL   INFO GRAPHIC   LIVE/IGTV   STORY

HOW ARE YOU FEELING TODAY?

DID YOU MAKE ANY SALES TODAY?

HOW MANY PEOPLE DID YOU TALK TO?

WHO ARE THEY?

WHO IS A WARM LEAD TODAY?

WHAT ARE YOU GOING TO DO TOMORROW
TO MOVE YOU FORWARDS?

SECOND 30 DAY CYCLE

M T W T F S S / WEEK 1 2 3 4 5

1 2 3 4 5 6 7 8 9 10 11 12 13 14 15 16 17
18 19 20 21 22 23 24 25 26 27 28 29 30 31

YOU ARE IN **TRUST ME**, HERE'S A PROMPT:
What would be your worst nightmare in business?

──────── WHAT WILL YOU WRITE FOR THIS PROMPT? ────────

──────── WHAT KEY POINTS WILL YOU TALK ABOUT? ────────

──────── WHAT FORMAT WILL YOU USE? ────────

POST   REEL   INFO GRAPHIC   LIVE/IGTV   STORY

HOW ARE YOU FEELING TODAY?

DID YOU MAKE ANY SALES TODAY?

HOW MANY PEOPLE DID YOU TALK TO?

WHO ARE THEY?

WHO IS A WARM LEAD TODAY?

WHAT ARE YOU GOING TO DO TOMORROW
TO MOVE YOU FORWARDS?

(SECOND) 30 DAY CYCLE

M T W T F S S / WEEK 1 2 3 4 5

1 2 3 4 5 6 7 8 9 10 11 12 13 14 15 16 17
18 19 20 21 22 23 24 25 26 27 28 29 30 31

_____

_____

_____

_____

YOU ARE IN **TRUST ME**, HERE'S A PROMPT:
Give your followers an 'either or' question to answer.

──────── WHAT WILL YOU WRITE FOR THIS PROMPT? ────────

──────── WHAT KEY POINTS WILL YOU TALK ABOUT? ────────

──────── WHAT FORMAT WILL YOU USE? ────────

POST   REEL   INFO GRAPHIC   LIVE/IGTV   STORY

HOW ARE YOU FEELING TODAY?

DID YOU MAKE ANY SALES TODAY?

HOW MANY PEOPLE DID YOU TALK TO?

WHO ARE THEY?

WHO IS A WARM LEAD TODAY?

WHAT ARE YOU GOING TO DO TOMORROW TO MOVE YOU FORWARDS?

10 Day Check In, how's it going?

HOW IS YOUR CONTENT PERFORMING?

BEST PERFORMING CONTENT?

LEAST PERFORMING CONTENT?

REACH	PROFILE VISITS	NEW FOLLOWERS	CONTENT INTERACTIONS	WEBSITE TAPS
◯	◯	◯	◯	◯

HOW DO YOU FEEL THINGS ARE GOING?

FREEWRITE

SECOND 30 DAY CYCLE

M T W T F S S / WEEK 1 2 3 4 5

1 2 3 4 5 6 7 8 9 10 11 12 13 14 15 16 17
18 19 20 21 22 23 24 25 26 27 28 29 30 31

YOU ARE IN **TRUST ME**, HERE'S A PROMPT:
Talk about something that happened right at the beginning of starting up your business.

———————— WHAT WILL YOU WRITE FOR THIS PROMPT? ————————

———————— WHAT KEY POINTS WILL YOU TALK ABOUT? ————————

———————— WHAT FORMAT WILL YOU USE? ————————

POST   REEL   INFO GRAPHIC   LIVE/IGTV   STORY

2ND 30 DAY CYCLE - DAY VIEW

HOW ARE YOU FEELING TODAY?

DID YOU MAKE ANY SALES TODAY?

HOW MANY PEOPLE DID YOU TALK TO?

WHO ARE THEY?

WHO IS A WARM LEAD TODAY?

WHAT ARE YOU GOING TO DO TOMORROW
TO MOVE YOU FORWARDS?

 SECOND 30 DAY CYCLE

M T W T F S S / WEEK 1 2 3 4 5

1 2 3 4 5 6 7 8 9 10 11 12 13 14 15 16 17
18 19 20 21 22 23 24 25 26 27 28 29 30 31

YOU ARE IN **TRUST ME**, HERE'S A PROMPT:
What's your big picture?

──────── WHAT WILL YOU WRITE FOR THIS PROMPT? ────────

──────── WHAT KEY POINTS WILL YOU TALK ABOUT? ────────

──────── WHAT FORMAT WILL YOU USE? ────────

POST   REEL   INFO GRAPHIC   LIVE/IGTV   STORY

HOW ARE YOU FEELING TODAY?

DID YOU MAKE ANY SALES TODAY?

HOW MANY PEOPLE DID YOU TALK TO?

WHO ARE THEY?

WHO IS A WARM LEAD TODAY?

WHAT ARE YOU GOING TO DO TOMORROW
TO MOVE YOU FORWARDS?

(SECOND) 30 DAY CYCLE

M T W T F S S / WEEK 1 2 3 4 5

1 2 3 4 5 6 7 8 9 10 11 12 13 14 15 16 17
18 19 20 21 22 23 24 25 26 27 28 29 30 31

YOU ARE IN **TRUST ME**, HERE'S A PROMPT:

*What makes you happy/ appeases your
personality in your business?*

———————— WHAT WILL YOU WRITE FOR THIS PROMPT? ————————

———————— WHAT KEY POINTS WILL YOU TALK ABOUT? ————————

———————— WHAT FORMAT WILL YOU USE? ————————

POST   REEL   INFO GRAPHIC   LIVE/IGTV   STORY

HOW ARE YOU FEELING TODAY?

DID YOU MAKE ANY SALES TODAY?

HOW MANY PEOPLE DID YOU TALK TO?

WHO ARE THEY?

WHO IS A WARM LEAD TODAY?

WHAT ARE YOU GOING TO DO TOMORROW TO MOVE YOU FORWARDS?

SECOND 30 DAY CYCLE

M T W T F S S / WEEK 1 2 3 4 5

1 2 3 4 5 6 7 8 9 10 11 12 13 14 15 16 17
18 19 20 21 22 23 24 25 26 27 28 29 30 31

YOU ARE IN **TRUST ME**, HERE'S A PROMPT:
How are you positioned in your industry?

──────── WHAT WILL YOU WRITE FOR THIS PROMPT? ────────

──────── WHAT KEY POINTS WILL YOU TALK ABOUT? ────────

──────── WHAT FORMAT WILL YOU USE? ────────

POST   REEL   INFO GRAPHIC   LIVE/IGTV   STORY

HOW ARE YOU FEELING TODAY?

DID YOU MAKE ANY SALES TODAY?

HOW MANY PEOPLE DID YOU TALK TO?

WHO ARE THEY?

WHO IS A WARM LEAD TODAY?

WHAT ARE YOU GOING TO DO TOMORROW
TO MOVE YOU FORWARDS?

SECOND 30 DAY CYCLE

M T W T F S S / WEEK 1 2 3 4 5

1 2 3 4 5 6 7 8 9 10 11 12 13 14 15 16 17
18 19 20 21 22 23 24 25 26 27 28 29 30 31

YOU ARE IN **TRUST ME**, HERE'S A PROMPT:
What do you say when you need to make someone feel better?

──────── WHAT WILL YOU WRITE FOR THIS PROMPT? ────────

──────── WHAT KEY POINTS WILL YOU TALK ABOUT? ────────

──────── WHAT FORMAT WILL YOU USE? ────────

POST   REEL   INFO GRAPHIC   LIVE/IGTV   STORY

HOW ARE YOU FEELING TODAY?

DID YOU MAKE ANY SALES TODAY?

HOW MANY PEOPLE DID YOU TALK TO?

WHO ARE THEY?

WHO IS A WARM LEAD TODAY?

WHAT ARE YOU GOING TO DO TOMORROW
TO MOVE YOU FORWARDS?

 SECOND 30 DAY CYCLE

M T W T F S S / WEEK 1 2 3 4 5

1 2 3 4 5 6 7 8 9 10 11 12 13 14 15 16 17
18 19 20 21 22 23 24 25 26 27 28 29 30 31

YOU ARE IN **TRUST ME**, HERE'S A PROMPT:
How much does your business overflow into being a part of you?

——————— WHAT WILL YOU WRITE FOR THIS PROMPT? ———————

——————— WHAT KEY POINTS WILL YOU TALK ABOUT? ———————

——————— WHAT FORMAT WILL YOU USE? ———————

POST   REEL   INFO GRAPHIC   LIVE/IGTV   STORY

HOW ARE YOU FEELING TODAY?

DID YOU MAKE ANY SALES TODAY?

HOW MANY PEOPLE DID YOU TALK TO?

WHO ARE THEY?

WHO IS A WARM LEAD TODAY?

WHAT ARE YOU GOING TO DO TOMORROW TO MOVE YOU FORWARDS?

(SECOND) 30 DAY CYCLE

M T W T F S S / WEEK 1 2 3 4 5

1 2 3 4 5 6 7 8 9 10 11 12 13 14 15 16 17
18 19 20 21 22 23 24 25 26 27 28 29 30 31

YOU ARE IN **TRUST ME**, HERE'S A PROMPT:
What is your ultimate purpose?

———————— WHAT WILL YOU WRITE FOR THIS PROMPT? ————————

———————— WHAT KEY POINTS WILL YOU TALK ABOUT? ————————

———————— WHAT FORMAT WILL YOU USE? ————————

POST   *REEL*   *INFO GRAPHIC*   *LIVE/IGTV*   *STORY*

HOW ARE YOU FEELING TODAY?

DID YOU MAKE ANY SALES TODAY?

HOW MANY PEOPLE DID YOU TALK TO?

WHO ARE THEY?

WHO IS A WARM LEAD TODAY?

WHAT ARE YOU GOING TO DO TOMORROW
TO MOVE YOU FORWARDS?

 SECOND 30 DAY CYCLE

M T W T F S S / WEEK 1 2 3 4 5

1 2 3 4 5 6 7 8 9 10 11 12 13 14 15 16 17
18 19 20 21 22 23 24 25 26 27 28 29 30 31

YOU ARE IN **TRUST ME**, HERE'S A PROMPT:
A testimonial based upon how you made them feel rather than what you did for them.

———————— WHAT WILL YOU WRITE FOR THIS PROMPT? ————————

———————— WHAT KEY POINTS WILL YOU TALK ABOUT? ————————

———————— WHAT FORMAT WILL YOU USE? ————————

POST   REEL   INFO GRAPHIC   LIVE/IGTV   STORY

HOW ARE YOU FEELING TODAY?

DID YOU MAKE ANY SALES TODAY?

HOW MANY PEOPLE DID YOU TALK TO?

WHO ARE THEY?

WHO IS A WARM LEAD TODAY?

WHAT ARE YOU GOING TO DO TOMORROW
TO MOVE YOU FORWARDS?

(SECOND) 30 DAY CYCLE

M T W T F S S / WEEK 1 2 3 4 5

1 2 3 4 5 6 7 8 9 10 11 12 13 14 15 16 17
18 19 20 21 22 23 24 25 26 27 28 29 30 31

_____

_____

_____

_____

YOU ARE IN **TRUST ME**, HERE'S A PROMPT:
What have you got for your customers at the moment?

——————————— WHAT WILL YOU WRITE FOR THIS PROMPT? ———————————

——————————— WHAT KEY POINTS WILL YOU TALK ABOUT? ———————————

——————————— WHAT FORMAT WILL YOU USE? ———————————

POST   REEL   INFO GRAPHIC   LIVE/IGTV   STORY

HOW ARE YOU FEELING TODAY?

DID YOU MAKE ANY SALES TODAY?

HOW MANY PEOPLE DID YOU TALK TO?

WHO ARE THEY?

WHO IS A WARM LEAD TODAY?

WHAT ARE YOU GOING TO DO TOMORROW
TO MOVE YOU FORWARDS?

(SECOND) 30 DAY CYCLE

M T W T F S S / WEEK 1 2 3 4 5

1 2 3 4 5 6 7 8 9 10 11 12 13 14 15 16 17
18 19 20 21 22 23 24 25 26 27 28 29 30 31

YOU ARE IN **TRUST ME**, HERE'S A PROMPT:
Break down your business into three bullet points.

──────── WHAT WILL YOU WRITE FOR THIS PROMPT? ────────

──────── WHAT KEY POINTS WILL YOU TALK ABOUT? ────────

──────── WHAT FORMAT WILL YOU USE? ────────

POST   REEL   INFO GRAPHIC   LIVE/IGTV   STORY

HOW ARE YOU FEELING TODAY?

DID YOU MAKE ANY SALES TODAY?

HOW MANY PEOPLE DID YOU TALK TO?

WHO ARE THEY?

WHO IS A WARM LEAD TODAY?

WHAT ARE YOU GOING TO DO TOMORROW TO MOVE YOU FORWARDS?

End of Your Second 30 Day Goal...

HOW MANY POSTS DID YOU DO?

( )

HOW MANY PEOPLE DID YOU CONNECT WITH
THAT WILL HELP YOUR BUSINESS?

( )

HOW MANY DAYS A WEEK DID
YOU POST STORIES?

( )

HOW MUCH TIME DID YOU SPEND
INTERACTING, NOT BROWSING?

WHAT PERCENTAGE GROWTH DID
YOU ACHIEVE THIS MONTH?

( )

HOW DID YOU FEEL ABOUT
INSTAGRAM THIS MONTH?

DO YOU NEED TO MUTE ANYONE?

FREEWRITE...

Onto the next
30 days...

Start of Your Third 30 Day Goal

M T W T F S S / WEEK 1 2 3 4 5

JAN   FEB   MAR   APR   MAY   JUN   JUL   AUG   SEP   OCT   NOV   DEC

M	T	W	T	F	S	S

WRITE YOUR GOAL HERE

HOW MANY POSTS DO YOU
WANT TO MAKE A WEEK?

HOW MANY PEOPLE DO YOU WANT TO CONNECT
WITH THAT WILL HELP YOUR BUSINESS?

HOW MANY DAYS A WEEK DO
YOU PLAN TO POST STORIES?

HOW MUCH TIME WILL YOU SPEND INTERACTING, NOT BROWSING?

WHAT PERCENTAGE GROWTH ARE YOU HOPING TO ACHIEVE THIS MONTH?

ANY OTHER GOALS?

FREEWRITE...

 THIRD 30 DAY CYCLE

M T W T F S S / WEEK 1 2 3 4 5

1 2 3 4 5 6 7 8 9 10 11 12 13 14 15 16 17
18 19 20 21 22 23 24 25 26 27 28 29 30 31

YOU ARE IN **TRUST ME**, HERE ARE YOUR PROMPTS:

Post: *What do you do that potential customers don't know they need yet?*
Email: *Explain what you have coming up and any nudges towards your upcoming product/services that you are campaigning or launching soon.*

──────── WHAT WILL YOU WRITE FOR THESE PROMPTS? ────────

──────── WHAT KEY POINTS WILL YOU TALK ABOUT? ────────

──────── WHAT FORMAT WILL YOU USE? ────────

POST   REEL   INFO GRAPHIC   LIVE/IGTV   STORY

HOW ARE YOU FEELING TODAY?

HOW MANY SALES DID YOU MAKE?

HOW MANY PEOPLE DID YOU TALK TO?

WHO ARE THEY?

WHO IS A WARM LEAD TODAY?

WHAT ARE YOU GOING TO DO TOMORROW
TO MAKE MORE SALES?

 THIRD 30 DAY CYCLE

M T W T F S S / WEEK 1 2 3 4 5

1 2 3 4 5 6 7 8 9 10 11 12 13 14 15 16 17
18 19 20 21 22 23 24 25 26 27 28 29 30 31

YOU ARE IN **TRUST ME**, HERE'S A PROMPT:
*Do you help people run away from pain or
run towards possibility?*

———— WHAT WILL YOU WRITE FOR THIS PROMPT? ————

———— WHAT KEY POINTS WILL YOU TALK ABOUT? ————

———— WHAT FORMAT WILL YOU USE? ————

POST   REEL   INFO GRAPHIC   LIVE/IGTV   STORY

HOW ARE YOU FEELING TODAY?

HOW MANY SALES DID YOU MAKE?

HOW MANY PEOPLE DID YOU TALK TO?

WHO ARE THEY?

WHO IS A WARM LEAD TODAY?

WHAT ARE YOU GOING TO DO TOMORROW
TO MAKE MORE SALES?

Order your next Content Planner now!

https://www.ingehunter.co.uk/content-planner

 THIRD 30 DAY CYCLE

M T W T F S S / WEEK 1 2 3 4 5

1 2 3 4 5 6 7 8 9 10 11 12 13 14 15 16 17
18 19 20 21 22 23 24 25 26 27 28 29 30 31

YOU ARE IN **TRUST ME**, HERE'S A PROMPT:
What do other people say about you in business?

———— WHAT WILL YOU WRITE FOR THIS PROMPT? ————

———— WHAT KEY POINTS WILL YOU TALK ABOUT? ————

———— WHAT FORMAT WILL YOU USE? ————

POST   REEL   INFO GRAPHIC   LIVE/IGTV   STORY

HOW ARE YOU FEELING TODAY?

HOW MANY SALES DID YOU MAKE?

HOW MANY PEOPLE DID YOU TALK TO?

WHO ARE THEY?

WHO IS A WARM LEAD TODAY?

WHAT ARE YOU GOING TO DO TOMORROW
TO MAKE MORE SALES?

(THIRD) 30 DAY CYCLE

M T W T F S S / WEEK 1 2 3 4 5

1 2 3 4 5 6 7 8 9 10 11 12 13 14 15 16 17
18 19 20 21 22 23 24 25 26 27 28 29 30 31

YOU ARE IN **TRUST ME**, HERE'S A PROMPT:
What's the biggest problem that your business has solved?

──────────── WHAT WILL YOU WRITE FOR THIS PROMPT? ────────────

──────────── WHAT KEY POINTS WILL YOU TALK ABOUT? ────────────

──────────── WHAT FORMAT WILL YOU USE? ────────────

POST   REEL   INFO GRAPHIC   LIVE/IGTV   STORY

HOW ARE YOU FEELING TODAY?

HOW MANY SALES DID YOU MAKE?

HOW MANY PEOPLE DID YOU TALK TO?

WHO ARE THEY?

WHO IS A WARM LEAD TODAY?

WHAT ARE YOU GOING TO DO TOMORROW
TO MAKE MORE SALES?

THIRD 30 DAY CYCLE

M T W T F S S / WEEK 1 2 3 4 5

1 2 3 4 5 6 7 8 9 10 11 12 13 14 15 16 17
18 19 20 21 22 23 24 25 26 27 28 29 30 31

YOU ARE IN **TRUST ME**, HERE'S A PROMPT:
What makes your business unique?

—————— WHAT WILL YOU WRITE FOR THIS PROMPT? ——————

—————— WHAT KEY POINTS WILL YOU TALK ABOUT? ——————

—————— WHAT FORMAT WILL YOU USE? ——————

POST   REEL   INFO GRAPHIC   LIVE/IGTV   STORY

HOW ARE YOU FEELING TODAY?

HOW MANY SALES DID YOU MAKE?

HOW MANY PEOPLE DID YOU TALK TO?

WHO ARE THEY?

WHO IS A WARM LEAD TODAY?

WHAT ARE YOU GOING TO DO TOMORROW
TO MAKE MORE SALES?

 THIRD 30 DAY CYCLE

M T W T F S S / WEEK 1 2 3 4 5

1 2 3 4 5 6 7 8 9 10 11 12 13 14 15 16 17
18 19 20 21 22 23 24 25 26 27 28 29 30 31

YOU ARE IN **TRUST ME**, HERE ARE YOUR PROMPTS:
Post: What is the big dream, big picture for anyone who buys your product/service?
Email: Talk about past customers or clients who you have loved and who your services/products are perfect for.

————————— WHAT WILL YOU WRITE FOR THESE PROMPTS? —————————

————————— WHAT KEY POINTS WILL YOU TALK ABOUT? —————————

————————— WHAT FORMAT WILL YOU USE? —————————

POST   REEL   INFO GRAPHIC   LIVE/IGTV   STORY

HOW ARE YOU FEELING TODAY?

HOW MANY SALES DID YOU MAKE?

HOW MANY PEOPLE DID YOU TALK TO?

WHO ARE THEY?

WHO IS A WARM LEAD TODAY?

WHAT ARE YOU GOING TO DO TOMORROW TO MAKE MORE SALES?

 THIRD 30 DAY CYCLE

M T W T F S S / WEEK 1 2 3 4 5

1 2 3 4 5 6 7 8 9 10 11 12 13 14 15 16 17
18 19 20 21 22 23 24 25 26 27 28 29 30 31

_____

_____

_____

_____

YOU ARE IN **BUY FROM ME**, HERE'S A PROMPT:
Talk about money and investment and address anything financial with your product/service.

---------------- WHAT WILL YOU WRITE FOR THIS PROMPT? ----------------

---------------- WHAT KEY POINTS WILL YOU TALK ABOUT? ----------------

---------------- WHAT FORMAT WILL YOU USE? ----------------

POST   REEL   INFO GRAPHIC   LIVE/IGTV   STORY

HOW ARE YOU FEELING TODAY?

HOW MANY SALES DID YOU MAKE?

HOW MANY PEOPLE DID YOU TALK TO?

WHO ARE THEY?

WHO IS A WARM LEAD TODAY?

WHAT ARE YOU GOING TO DO TOMORROW
TO MAKE MORE SALES?

(THIRD) 30 DAY CYCLE

M T W T F S S / WEEK 1 2 3 4 5

1 2 3 4 5 6 7 8 9 10 11 12 13 14 15 16 17
18 19 20 21 22 23 24 25 26 27 28 29 30 31

YOU ARE IN **BUY FROM ME**, HERE'S A PROMPT:
What problems do you like to solve in your business?

—————————— WHAT WILL YOU WRITE FOR THIS PROMPT? ——————————

—————————— WHAT KEY POINTS WILL YOU TALK ABOUT? ——————————

—————————— WHAT FORMAT WILL YOU USE? ——————————

POST   REEL   INFO GRAPHIC   LIVE/IGTV   STORY

HOW ARE YOU FEELING TODAY?

HOW MANY SALES DID YOU MAKE?

HOW MANY PEOPLE DID YOU TALK TO?

WHO ARE THEY?

WHO IS A WARM LEAD TODAY?

WHAT ARE YOU GOING TO DO TOMORROW
TO MAKE MORE SALES?

 THIRD 30 DAY CYCLE

M T W T F S S / WEEK 1 2 3 4 5

1 2 3 4 5 6 7 8 9 10 11 12 13 14 15 16 17
18 19 20 21 22 23 24 25 26 27 28 29 30 31

YOU ARE IN **BUY FROM ME**, HERE'S A PROMPT:
What are you selling, what do you want to focus peoples attention onto?

———— WHAT WILL YOU WRITE FOR THIS PROMPT? ————

———— WHAT KEY POINTS WILL YOU TALK ABOUT? ————

———— WHAT FORMAT WILL YOU USE? ————

POST   REEL   INFO GRAPHIC   LIVE/IGTV   STORY

HOW ARE YOU FEELING TODAY?

HOW MANY SALES DID YOU MAKE?

HOW MANY PEOPLE DID YOU TALK TO?

WHO ARE THEY?

WHO IS A WARM LEAD TODAY?

WHAT ARE YOU GOING TO DO TOMORROW
TO MAKE MORE SALES?

(THIRD) 30 DAY CYCLE

M T W T F S S / WEEK 1 2 3 4 5

1 2 3 4 5 6 7 8 9 10 11 12 13 14 15 16 17
18 19 20 21 22 23 24 25 26 27 28 29 30 31

YOU ARE IN **BUY FROM ME**, HERE'S A PROMPT:
What kind of personality does your ideal client have?

———— WHAT WILL YOU WRITE FOR THIS PROMPT? ————

———— WHAT KEY POINTS WILL YOU TALK ABOUT? ————

———— WHAT FORMAT WILL YOU USE? ————

POST   REEL   INFO GRAPHIC   LIVE/IGTV   STORY

HOW ARE YOU FEELING TODAY?

HOW MANY SALES DID YOU MAKE?

HOW MANY PEOPLE DID YOU TALK TO?

WHO ARE THEY?

WHO IS A WARM LEAD TODAY?

WHAT ARE YOU GOING TO DO TOMORROW
TO MAKE MORE SALES?

10 Day Check In, how's it going?

HOW IS YOUR CONTENT PERFORMING?

BEST PERFORMING CONTENT?

LEAST PERFORMING CONTENT?

REACH	PROFILE VISITS	NEW FOLLOWERS	CONTENT INTERACTIONS	WEBSITE TAPS
◯	◯	◯	◯	◯

HOW DO YOU FEEL THINGS ARE GOING?

FREEWRITE

 THIRD 30 DAY CYCLE

M T W T F S S / WEEK 1 2 3 4 5

1 2 3 4 5 6 7 8 9 10 11 12 13 14 15 16 17
18 19 20 21 22 23 24 25 26 27 28 29 30 31

YOU ARE IN **BUY FROM ME**, HERE ARE YOUR PROMPTS:
Post: What are you selling, what do you want to focus peoples attention onto?
Email: Detail why you do what you and why you're passionate about your product/service.

--------- WHAT WILL YOU WRITE FOR THESE PROMPTS? ---------

--------- WHAT KEY POINTS WILL YOU TALK ABOUT? ---------

--------- WHAT FORMAT WILL YOU USE? ---------

POST   REEL   INFO GRAPHIC   LIVE/IGTV   STORY

HOW ARE YOU FEELING TODAY?

HOW MANY SALES DID YOU MAKE?

HOW MANY PEOPLE DID YOU TALK TO?

WHO ARE THEY?

WHO IS A WARM LEAD TODAY?

WHAT ARE YOU GOING TO DO TOMORROW
TO MAKE MORE SALES?

(THIRD) 30 DAY CYCLE

M T W T F S S / WEEK 1 2 3 4 5

1 2 3 4 5 6 7 8 9 10 11 12 13 14 15 16 17
18 19 20 21 22 23 24 25 26 27 28 29 30 31

YOU ARE IN **BUY FROM ME**, HERE'S A PROMPT:
Do you feel passionate about your business?
How does that make you feel?

--- WHAT WILL YOU WRITE FOR THIS PROMPT? ---

--- WHAT KEY POINTS WILL YOU TALK ABOUT? ---

--- WHAT FORMAT WILL YOU USE? ---

POST   REEL   INFO GRAPHIC   LIVE/IGTV   STORY

HOW ARE YOU FEELING TODAY?

HOW MANY SALES DID YOU MAKE?

HOW MANY PEOPLE DID YOU TALK TO?

WHO ARE THEY?

WHO IS A WARM LEAD TODAY?

WHAT ARE YOU GOING TO DO TOMORROW
TO MAKE MORE SALES?

(THIRD) 30 DAY CYCLE

M T W T F S S / WEEK 1 2 3 4 5

1 2 3 4 5 6 7 8 9 10 11 12 13 14 15 16 17
18 19 20 21 22 23 24 25 26 27 28 29 30 31

YOU ARE IN **BUY FROM ME**, HERE'S A PROMPT:
What makes you care about what you do?

WHAT WILL YOU WRITE FOR THIS PROMPT?

WHAT KEY POINTS WILL YOU TALK ABOUT?

WHAT FORMAT WILL YOU USE?

POST   REEL   INFO GRAPHIC   LIVE/IGTV   STORY

HOW ARE YOU FEELING TODAY?

HOW MANY SALES DID YOU MAKE?

HOW MANY PEOPLE DID YOU TALK TO?

WHO ARE THEY?

WHO IS A WARM LEAD TODAY?

WHAT ARE YOU GOING TO DO TOMORROW
TO MAKE MORE SALES?

(THIRD) 30 DAY CYCLE

M T W T F S S / WEEK 1 2 3 4 5

1 2 3 4 5 6 7 8 9 10 11 12 13 14 15 16 17
18 19 20 21 22 23 24 25 26 27 28 29 30 31

_____

_____

_____

_____

YOU ARE IN **BUY FROM ME**, HERE'S A PROMPT:
Tell us about your journey of business conception to launch?

──────── WHAT WILL YOU WRITE FOR THIS PROMPT? ────────

──────── WHAT KEY POINTS WILL YOU TALK ABOUT? ────────

──────── WHAT FORMAT WILL YOU USE? ────────

POST   REEL   INFO GRAPHIC   LIVE/IGTV   STORY

HOW ARE YOU FEELING TODAY?

HOW MANY SALES DID YOU MAKE?

HOW MANY PEOPLE DID YOU TALK TO?

WHO ARE THEY?

WHO IS A WARM LEAD TODAY?

WHAT ARE YOU GOING TO DO TOMORROW TO MAKE MORE SALES?

THIRD 30 DAY CYCLE

M T W T F S S / WEEK 1 2 3 4 5

1 2 3 4 5 6 7 8 9 10 11 12 13 14 15 16 17
18 19 20 21 22 23 24 25 26 27 28 29 30 31

YOU ARE IN **BUY FROM ME**, HERE'S A PROMPT:
What is your favourite thing about your kind of clients?

──────── WHAT WILL YOU WRITE FOR THIS PROMPT? ────────

──────── WHAT KEY POINTS WILL YOU TALK ABOUT? ────────

──────── WHAT FORMAT WILL YOU USE? ────────

POST   REEL   INFO GRAPHIC   LIVE/IGTV   STORY

HOW ARE YOU FEELING TODAY?

HOW MANY SALES DID YOU MAKE?

HOW MANY PEOPLE DID YOU TALK TO?

WHO ARE THEY?

WHO IS A WARM LEAD TODAY?

WHAT ARE YOU GOING TO DO TOMORROW
TO MAKE MORE SALES?

THIRD 30 DAY CYCLE

M T W T F S S / WEEK 1 2 3 4 5

1 2 3 4 5 6 7 8 9 10 11 12 13 14 15 16 17
18 19 20 21 22 23 24 25 26 27 28 29 30 31

YOU ARE IN **BUY FROM ME**, HERE ARE YOUR PROMPTS:
Post: Tell us to get in touch if we are interested in your product/ service.
Email: Explain how people most like to work with you or how they like to use your products.

—————————— WHAT WILL YOU WRITE FOR THESE PROMPTS? ——————————

—————————— WHAT KEY POINTS WILL YOU TALK ABOUT? ——————————

—————————— WHAT FORMAT WILL YOU USE? ——————————

POST   REEL   INFO GRAPHIC   LIVE/IGTV   STORY

HOW ARE YOU FEELING TODAY?

HOW MANY SALES DID YOU MAKE?

HOW MANY PEOPLE DID YOU TALK TO?

WHO ARE THEY?

WHO IS A WARM LEAD TODAY?

WHAT ARE YOU GOING TO DO TOMORROW
TO MAKE MORE SALES?

(THIRD) 30 DAY CYCLE

M T W T F S S / WEEK 1 2 3 4 5

1 2 3 4 5 6 7 8 9 10 11 12 13 14 15 16 17
18 19 20 21 22 23 24 25 26 27 28 29 30 31

YOU ARE IN **BUY FROM ME**, HERE'S A PROMPT:
How do you keep yourself going?

—————— WHAT WILL YOU WRITE FOR THIS PROMPT? ——————

—————— WHAT KEY POINTS WILL YOU TALK ABOUT? ——————

—————— WHAT FORMAT WILL YOU USE? ——————

POST   REEL   INFO GRAPHIC   LIVE/IGTV   STORY

HOW ARE YOU FEELING TODAY?

HOW MANY SALES DID YOU MAKE?

HOW MANY PEOPLE DID YOU TALK TO?

WHO ARE THEY?

WHO IS A WARM LEAD TODAY?

WHAT ARE YOU GOING TO DO TOMORROW
TO MAKE MORE SALES?

(THIRD) 30 DAY CYCLE

M T W T F S S / WEEK 1 2 3 4 5

1 2 3 4 5 6 7 8 9 10 11 12 13 14 15 16 17
18 19 20 21 22 23 24 25 26 27 28 29 30 31

YOU ARE IN **BUY FROM ME**, HERE'S A PROMPT:
What are you most excited about in your service/ product?

──────────── HOW WILL YOU WRITE FOR THIS PROMPT? ────────────

──────────── WHAT KEY POINTS WILL YOU TALK ABOUT? ────────────

──────────── WHAT FORMAT WILL YOU USE? ────────────

POST   REEL   INFO GRAPHIC   LIVE/IGTV   STORY

HOW ARE YOU FEELING TODAY?

HOW MANY SALES DID YOU MAKE?

HOW MANY PEOPLE DID YOU TALK TO?

WHO ARE THEY?

WHO IS A WARM LEAD TODAY?

WHAT ARE YOU GOING TO DO TOMORROW TO MAKE MORE SALES?

(THIRD) 30 DAY CYCLE

M T W T F S S / WEEK 1 2 3 4 5

1 2 3 4 5 6 7 8 9 10 11 12 13 14 15 16 17
18 19 20 21 22 23 24 25 26 27 28 29 30 31

YOU ARE IN **BUY FROM ME**, HERE'S A PROMPT:
How do people normally buy from you?

──────── WHAT WILL YOU WRITE FOR THIS PROMPT? ────────

──────── WHAT KEY POINTS WILL YOU TALK ABOUT? ────────

──────── WHAT FORMAT WILL YOU USE? ────────

POST   REEL   INFO GRAPHIC   LIVE/IGTV   STORY

HOW ARE YOU FEELING TODAY?

HOW MANY SALES DID YOU MAKE?

HOW MANY PEOPLE DID YOU TALK TO?

WHO ARE THEY?

WHO IS A WARM LEAD TODAY?

WHAT ARE YOU GOING TO DO TOMORROW
TO MAKE MORE SALES?

(THIRD) 30 DAY CYCLE

M T W T F S S / WEEK 1 2 3 4 5

1 2 3 4 5 6 7 8 9 10 11 12 13 14 15 16 17
18 19 20 21 22 23 24 25 26 27 28 29 30 31

YOU ARE IN **BUY FROM ME**, HERE ARE YOUR PROMPTS:

Post: How do you feel about the thing you're selling?

Email: Email everyone with details of your available products/ services and a direction to your sales page or shop on your website.

———— WHAT WILL YOU WRITE FOR THESE PROMPTS? ————

———— WHAT KEY POINTS WILL YOU TALK ABOUT? ————

———— WHAT FORMAT WILL YOU USE? ————

POST   REEL   INFO GRAPHIC   LIVE/IGTV   STORY

HOW ARE YOU FEELING TODAY?

HOW MANY SALES DID YOU MAKE?

HOW MANY PEOPLE DID YOU TALK TO?

WHO ARE THEY?

WHO IS A WARM LEAD TODAY?

WHAT ARE YOU GOING TO DO TOMORROW
TO MAKE MORE SALES?

10 Day Check In, how's it going?

HOW IS YOUR CONTENT PERFORMING?

BEST PERFORMING CONTENT?

LEAST PERFORMING CONTENT?

REACH	PROFILE VISITS	NEW FOLLOWERS	CONTENT INTERACTIONS	WEBSITE TAPS
◯	◯	◯	◯	◯

HOW DO YOU FEEL THINGS ARE GOING?

FREEWRITE

 THIRD 30 DAY CYCLE

M T W T F S S / WEEK 1 2 3 4 5

1 2 3 4 5 6 7 8 9 10 11 12 13 14 15 16 17
18 19 20 21 22 23 24 25 26 27 28 29 30 31

YOU ARE IN **BUY FROM ME**, HERE'S A PROMPT:
When can we get hold of your product/ access your service?

──────── WHAT WILL YOU WRITE FOR THIS PROMPT? ────────

──────── WHAT KEY POINTS WILL YOU TALK ABOUT? ────────

──────── WHAT FORMAT WILL YOU USE? ────────

POST   REEL   INFO GRAPHIC   LIVE/IGTV   STORY

HOW ARE YOU FEELING TODAY?

HOW MANY SALES DID YOU MAKE?

HOW MANY PEOPLE DID YOU TALK TO?

WHO ARE THEY?

WHO IS A WARM LEAD TODAY?

WHAT ARE YOU GOING TO DO TOMORROW
TO MAKE MORE SALES?

(THIRD) 30 DAY CYCLE

M T W T F S S / WEEK 1 2 3 4 5

1 2 3 4 5 6 7 8 9 10 11 12 13 14 15 16 17
18 19 20 21 22 23 24 25 26 27 28 29 30 31

YOU ARE IN **BUY FROM ME**, HERE'S A PROMPT:
Who is your product/ service good for?

──────── WHAT WILL YOU WRITE FOR THIS PROMPT? ────────

──────── WHAT KEY POINTS WILL YOU TALK ABOUT? ────────

──────── WHAT FORMAT WILL YOU USE? ────────

POST   REEL   INFO GRAPHIC   LIVE/IGTV   STORY

HOW ARE YOU FEELING TODAY?

HOW MANY SALES DID YOU MAKE?

HOW MANY PEOPLE DID YOU TALK TO?

WHO ARE THEY?

WHO IS A WARM LEAD TODAY?

WHAT ARE YOU GOING TO DO TOMORROW TO MAKE MORE SALES?

 THIRD 30 DAY CYCLE

M T W T F S S / WEEK 1 2 3 4 5

1 2 3 4 5 6 7 8 9 10 11 12 13 14 15 16 17
18 19 20 21 22 23 24 25 26 27 28 29 30 31

_____

_____

_____

_____

YOU ARE IN **BUY FROM ME**, HERE ARE YOUR PROMPTS:
Post: Who is your product/ service good for?
Email: Tell us what it's about and explain in more detail any
bonuses you have.

———————— WHAT WILL YOU WRITE FOR THESE PROMPTS? ————————

———————— WHAT KEY POINTS WILL YOU TALK ABOUT? ————————

———————— WHAT FORMAT WILL YOU USE? ————————

POST   REEL   INFO GRAPHIC   LIVE/IGTV   STORY

HOW ARE YOU FEELING TODAY?

HOW MANY SALES DID YOU MAKE?

HOW MANY PEOPLE DID YOU TALK TO?

WHO ARE THEY?

WHO IS A WARM LEAD TODAY?

WHAT ARE YOU GOING TO DO TOMORROW
TO MAKE MORE SALES?

THIRD 30 DAY CYCLE

M T W T F S S / WEEK 1 2 3 4 5

1 2 3 4 5 6 7 8 9 10 11 12 13 14 15 16 17
18 19 20 21 22 23 24 25 26 27 28 29 30 31

_____

_____

_____

_____

YOU ARE IN **BUY FROM ME**, HERE ARE YOUR PROMPTS:
Post: *What specifically are you selling? Break it down.*
Email: *Email telling us the story of conception of your product/ service and that people can get in touch to ask questions.*

──────── WHAT WILL YOU WRITE FOR THESE PROMPTS? ────────

──────── WHAT KEY POINTS WILL YOU TALK ABOUT? ────────

──────── WHAT FORMAT WILL YOU USE? ────────

POST   REEL   INFO GRAPHIC   LIVE/IGTV   STORY

HOW ARE YOU FEELING TODAY?

HOW MANY SALES DID YOU MAKE?

HOW MANY PEOPLE DID YOU TALK TO?

WHO ARE THEY?

WHO IS A WARM LEAD TODAY?

WHAT ARE YOU GOING TO DO TOMORROW
TO MAKE MORE SALES?

 THIRD 30 DAY CYCLE

M T W T F S S / WEEK 1 2 3 4 5

1 2 3 4 5 6 7 8 9 10 11 12 13 14 15 16 17
18 19 20 21 22 23 24 25 26 27 28 29 30 31

_____

_____

_____

_____

YOU ARE IN **BUY FROM ME**, HERE ARE YOUR PROMPTS:
Post: Why are you selling what you're selling?
Email: Explain the process of buying or working with you and
how to get in touch.

──────────── WHAT WILL YOU WRITE FOR THESE PROMPTS? ────────────

──────────── WHAT KEY POINTS WILL YOU TALK ABOUT? ────────────

──────────── WHAT FORMAT WILL YOU USE? ────────────

POST   REEL   INFO GRAPHIC   LIVE/IGTV   STORY

HOW ARE YOU FEELING TODAY?

HOW MANY SALES DID YOU MAKE?

HOW MANY PEOPLE DID YOU TALK TO?

WHO ARE THEY?

WHO IS A WARM LEAD TODAY?

WHAT ARE YOU GOING TO DO TOMORROW
TO MAKE MORE SALES?

 THIRD 30 DAY CYCLE

M T W T F S S / WEEK 1 2 3 4 5

1 2 3 4 5 6 7 8 9 10 11 12 13 14 15 16 17
18 19 20 21 22 23 24 25 26 27 28 29 30 31

YOU ARE IN **BUY FROM ME**, HERE ARE YOUR PROMPTS:
Post: Talk about the potential possibilities after they buy from you.
Email: Email saying how amazing people feel after they have worked with you/ bought your product and how to get in touch.

———————— WHAT WILL YOU WRITE FOR THESE PROMPTS? ————————

———————— WHAT KEY POINTS WILL YOU TALK ABOUT? ————————

———————— WHAT FORMAT WILL YOU USE? ————————

POST   REEL   INFO GRAPHIC   LIVE/IGTV   STORY

HOW ARE YOU FEELING TODAY?

HOW MANY SALES DID YOU MAKE?

HOW MANY PEOPLE DID YOU TALK TO?

WHO ARE THEY?

WHO IS A WARM LEAD TODAY?

WHAT ARE YOU GOING TO DO TOMORROW
TO MAKE MORE SALES?

THIRD 30 DAY CYCLE

M T W T F S S / WEEK 1 2 3 4 5

1 2 3 4 5 6 7 8 9 10 11 12 13 14 15 16 17
18 19 20 21 22 23 24 25 26 27 28 29 30 31

YOU ARE IN **BUY FROM ME**, HERE ARE YOUR PROMPTS:
Post: Talk about the pain/ problems that your product/ service solves.
Email: Email showing your testimonials and details of who buys from you and what they say and how to get in touch.

——————— WHAT WILL YOU WRITE FOR THESE PROMPTS? ———————

——————— WHAT KEY POINTS WILL YOU TALK ABOUT? ———————

——————— WHAT FORMAT WILL YOU USE? ———————

POST   REEL   INFO GRAPHIC   LIVE/IGTV   STORY

HOW ARE YOU FEELING TODAY?

HOW MANY SALES DID YOU MAKE?

HOW MANY PEOPLE DID YOU TALK TO?

WHO ARE THEY?

WHO IS A WARM LEAD TODAY?

WHAT ARE YOU GOING TO DO TOMORROW
TO MAKE MORE SALES?

THIRD 30 DAY CYCLE

M T W T F S S / WEEK 1 2 3 4 5

1 2 3 4 5 6 7 8 9 10 11 12 13 14 15 16 17
18 19 20 21 22 23 24 25 26 27 28 29 30 31

_____

_____

_____

_____

_____

YOU ARE IN **BUY FROM ME**, HERE ARE YOUR PROMPTS:
Post: Problems that you notice in your industry that your product/ service fixes.
Email: Explain the common FAQs you've had and addressing any thing
people have said as to why they haven't bought yet and how to get in touch.

————————— WHAT WILL YOU WRITE FOR THESE PROMPTS? —————————

————————— WHAT KEY POINTS WILL YOU TALK ABOUT? —————————

————————— WHAT FORMAT WILL YOU USE? —————————

POST   REEL   INFO GRAPHIC   LIVE/IGTV   STORY

HOW ARE YOU FEELING TODAY?

HOW MANY SALES DID YOU MAKE?

HOW MANY PEOPLE DID YOU TALK TO?

WHO ARE THEY?

WHO IS A WARM LEAD TODAY?

WHAT ARE YOU GOING TO DO TOMORROW
TO MAKE MORE SALES?

 THIRD 30 DAY CYCLE

| M | T | W | T | F | S | S | / | WEEK | 1 | 2 | 3 | 4 | 5 |

1 2 3 4 5 6 7 8 9 10 11 12 13 14 15 16 17
18 19 20 21 22 23 24 25 26 27 28 29 30 31

_____

_____

_____

_____

YOU ARE IN **BUY FROM ME**, HERE ARE YOUR PROMPTS:
Post: Address any barriers to working with your business.
Email: Discuss anything time sensitive or limiting about your product/ service to encourage them to buy now.

───────── WHAT WILL YOU WRITE FOR THESE PROMPTS? ─────────

───────── WHAT KEY POINTS WILL YOU TALK ABOUT? ─────────

───────── WHAT FORMAT WILL YOU USE? ─────────

POST   REEL   INFO GRAPHIC   LIVE/IGTV   STORY

HOW ARE YOU FEELING TODAY?

HOW MANY SALES DID YOU MAKE?

HOW MANY PEOPLE DID YOU TALK TO?

WHO ARE THEY?

WHO IS A WARM LEAD TODAY?

WHAT ARE YOU GOING TO DO TOMORROW
TO MAKE MORE SALES?

THIRD 30 DAY CYCLE

M T W T F S S / WEEK 1 2 3 4 5

1 2 3 4 5 6 7 8 9 10 11 12 13 14 15 16 17
18 19 20 21 22 23 24 25 26 27 28 29 30 31

YOU ARE IN **BUY FROM ME**, HERE ARE YOUR PROMPTS:

Post: *Talk about why you're passionate about the thing you're selling.*
Email: *Email with your last pitch.*

———— WHAT WILL YOU WRITE FOR THESE PROMPTS? ————

———— WHAT KEY POINTS WILL YOU TALK ABOUT? ————

———— WHAT FORMAT WILL YOU USE? ————

POST   REEL   INFO GRAPHIC   LIVE/IGTV   STORY

HOW ARE YOU FEELING TODAY?

HOW MANY SALES DID YOU MAKE?

HOW MANY PEOPLE DID YOU TALK TO?

WHO ARE THEY?

WHO IS A WARM LEAD TODAY?

WHAT ARE YOU GOING TO DO TOMORROW TO MAKE MORE SALES?

10 Day Check In, how's it going?

HOW IS YOUR CONTENT PERFORMING?

BEST PERFORMING CONTENT?

LEAST PERFORMING CONTENT?

REACH	PROFILE VISITS	NEW FOLLOWERS	CONTENT INTERACTIONS	WEBSITE TAPS
◯	◯	◯	◯	◯

HOW DO YOU FEEL THINGS ARE GOING?

FREEWRITE

End of Your Third 30 Day Goal

————— HOW MANY POSTS DID YOU DO? —————

◯

————— HOW MANY PEOPLE DID YOU CONNECT WITH
THAT WILL HELP YOUR BUSINESS? —————

◯

————— HOW MANY DAYS A WEEK DID
YOU POST STORIES? —————

◯

————— HOW MUCH TIME DID YOU SPEND
INTERACTING, NOT BROWSING? —————

————— WHAT PERCENTAGE GROWTH DID
YOU ACHIEVE THIS MONTH? —————

◯

HOW DID YOU FEEL ABOUT INSTAGRAM THIS MONTH?

DO YOU NEED TO MUTE ANYONE?

FREEWRITE...

Let's Recap on Your 90 Day Goal

M T W T F S S / WEEK 1 2 3 4 5

JAN FEB MAR APR MAY JUN JUL AUG SEP OCT NOV DEC

HOW DO YOU FEEL?

DID YOU ACHIEVE YOUR GOALS?

DID YOU ACHIEVE YOUR FINANCIAL GOAL?

ORIGINAL GOAL **ACTUAL AMOUNT**

DID YOU ACHIEVE YOUR IMPACT GOAL?

HOW DO YOU FEEL ABOUT YOUR BUSINESS AFTER THE 90 DAYS?

WHAT WILL YOU CHANGE / DO IN THE FUTURE?

Space to Track Your Leads...

NAME	PLACE OF CONTACT	ANY NOTES	SALE

Space to Track Your Sales...

☐   ☐   ☐

☐   ☐   ☐

☐   ☐   ☐

☐   ☐   ☐

☐   ☐   ☐

☐   ☐   ☐

☐   ☐   ☐

☐   ☐   ☐

☐   ☐   ☐

☐   ☐   ☐

☐   ☐   ☐

☐   ☐   ☐

☐   ☐   ☐

Printed in Great Britain
by Amazon

70278384R00140